ROYAL COL

C000203055

The Royal Court Theatre presents

SPUR OF THE MOMENT

by **Anya Reiss**

First performance at The Royal Court Jerwood Theatre Upstairs, Sloane Square, London
on Wednesday 14 July 2010.

JERWOOD
NEW PLAYWRIGHTS

Supported by the Jerwood Charitable Foundation

SPUR OF THE MOMENT

by Anya Reiss

in order of appearance
Delilah Evans **Shannon Tarbet**
Emma M **Jordan Loughran**
Emma G **Yasmin Paige**
Naomi **Rosie Day**
Daniel Mast **James McArdle**
Nick Evans **Kevin Doyle**
Vicky Evans **Sharon Small**
Leonie Fowler **Aisling Loftus**

Director **Jeremy Herrin**
Designer **Max Jones**
Lighting **Malcolm Rippeth**
Sound **Ian Dickinson for Autograph**
Casting Director **Julia Horan**
Assistant Director **Monique Sterling**
Production Manager **Tariq Rifaat**
Stage Managers **Kate McDowell, Fran O'Donnell**
Costume Supervisor **Iona Kenrick**
Stage Management Placement **Adriana Ludé**
Set Built by **Weld-Fab Stage Engineering Ltd, RCT Stage Dept**

THE COMPANY

ANYA REISS (Writer)

Born and brought up in London, Anya took part in a half-term holiday writing course at the Royal Court when she was 14 and went on to join the Young Writer's Programme. While on the Studio Group she wrote Spur of the Moment, which was used in a 20 minute reading celebrating the Arts' Council's Night Less Ordinary scheme. Anya is currently studying for her A-Levels.

ROSIE DAY (Naomi)

THEATRE INCLUDES: Summerfolk, The Winter's Tale, Playboy of the Western World (National); Les Miserables (West End).

TELEVISION INCLUDES: Summer in Transylvania, Half Moon Investigations, Doctors, The Large Family, Harley Street, Dead Gorgeous, My Life as a Popat, Romantics, Pants on Fire, Bernard's Watch, Family Affairs, In Deep, Big Train, Black Books, Hope and Glory.

FILM INCLUDES: Annie's Box.

RADIO INCLUDES: Mother Spy, The Christmas Angel, Why the Whales Came.

KEVIN DOYLE (Nick Evans)

THEATRE INCLUDES: The White Guard, Mutabilitie (National); For King and Country (Touring Partnership); Three in the Back, Two in the Head, The Mob, A Hole in the Top of the World (Orange Tree); Comedy of Errors (Southampton); Henry V, Coriolanus, A Midsummer Night's Dream, Artistes and Admirers, Romeo & Juliet, A Woman Killed with Kindness, Henry IV Parts I & II, Kissing the Pope, Twelfth Night, The Plantagenets, The Plain Dealer (RSC); The Crucible (West Yorkshire Playhouse); Much Ado About Nothing (UK tour); Hamlet (Haworth Festival, New Jersey); Thérèse Raquin (Chichester Minerva Studio); Othello (Bristol Old Vic); The Admirable Crichton, Great Expectations, Cymbeline (Manchester Royal Exchange); A Man for All Seasons (Great Eastern Stage); Hay Fever, The Miser (Cambridge Theatre Company).

TELEVISION INCLUDES: Downton Abbey, Law & Order, Vexed, Survivors, Five Days, Paradox, Silent Witness, The Tudors, Till We Die, George Gently, Sleep with Me, Heartbeat, Belle de jour, Drop Dead Gorgeous, Dalziel & Pascoe, Casualty, The Royal, New Street Law, The Brief, Brief Encounters, Afterlife, Big Dippers, The Rotters Club, Blackpool, Midsomer Murders, Family Business, Murphy's Law, Silent Witness, The Lakes, Holby City, At Home with the Braithwaites, Badger.

FILM INCLUDES: Good, The Libertine, A Social Call, A Midsummer Night's Dream..

IAN DICKINSON (Sound Designer)

FOR THE ROYAL COURT: Jerusalem (& Apollo Theatre, West End), Wig Out!, Now Or Later, Gone Too Far! The Family Plays, Rhinoceros, My Child, The Eleventh Capital, The Seagull (& Broadway), Krapp's Last Tape, Piano/Forte, Rock 'n' Roll (& Duke of York's/Broadway), Motortown, Rainbow Kiss, The Winterling, Alice Trilogy, Fewer Emergencies, Way to Heaven, The Woman Before, Stoning Mary (& Drum Theatre, Plymouth), Breathing Corpses, Wild East, Dumb Show, Shining City (& Gate, Dublin), Lucky Dog, Blest Be the Tie (with Talawa), Ladybird, Notes on Falling Leaves, Loyal Women, The Sugar Syndrome, Blood, Playing the Victim (with Told By an Idiot), Fallout, Flesh Wound, Hitchcock Blonde (& Lyric), Black Milk, Crazyblackmuthafuckin'self, Caryl Churchill Shorts, Push Up, Fucking Games, Herons.

OTHER THEATRE INCLUDES: After the Dance, All's Well That Ends Well, Death & The King's Horseman, Harper Regan, The Hothouse, Pillars of the Community (National); The Misanthrope (Comedy, West End); Little Voice (Vaudeville, West End); Mrs Klein (Almeida); 1984, Macbeth, Port, As You Like It, Poor Superman, Martin Yesterday, Fast Food, Coyote Ugly (Royal Exchange, Manchester); Testing The Echo, King Of Hearts (Out of Joint); Love & Money, Senora Carrar's Rifles (Young Vic); Othello, Much Ado About Nothing (redesign), Night of the Soul (RSC); A Few Good Men (Theatre Royal, Haymarket); Dr Faustus (Chichester Festival Theatre); The Magic Carpet (Lyric Hammersmith); Under the Curse, Eyes of the Kappa (Gate); Crime & Punishment in Dalston (Arcola); Search & Destroy (New End); The Whore's Dream (RSC/Edinburgh).

Having previously being resident at the Royal Court Theatre for many years Ian joined the Autograph design team in 2009, Autograph are a leading British sound design and equipment hire company, responsible for numerous theatre productions at home and abroad.

JEREMY HERRIN (Director)

FOR THE ROYAL COURT: Off The Endz, The Priory, Tusk Tusk, The Vertical Hour, That Face (& Duke of York's).

OTHER THEATRE INCLUDES: Marble (Abbey, Dublin); The Family Reunion (Donmar); Blackbird (Market Theatre, Johannesburg); Statement of Regret (National); Sudden Collapses in Public Places, The Boy on the Swing, Gathered Dust and Dead Skin, The Lovers, Our Kind of Fun, Toast, Dirty Nets, Smack Family Robinson, Attachments, From the Underworld, The Last Post, Personal Belongings, ne1, Knives in Hens (Live Theatre).

FOR THE ROYAL COURT, AS ASSISTANT DIRECTOR: My Night with Reg, Babies, Thyestes, The Kitchen.

FILM & TELEVISION INCLUDES: Linked, Dead Terry, Warmth, Cold Calling.

Jeremy is Deputy Artistic Director of the Royal Court.

MAX JONES (Designer)

THEATRE INCLUDES: A Small Family Business, Mary Stuart, Measure For Measure, Two Princes, The Mabinogion, Porth y Byddar, The Grapes of Wrath (Theatre Clwyd); Party (The Arts Theatre); Mad Forest (BAC); The Caretaker (Citizens' Theatre, Glasgow), Dumb Show (New Vic Theatre, Stoke); Sweeney Todd (Welsh National Youth Opera); Ryan and Ronnie (Script Cymru); Salt Meets Wound (Theatre 503).

AWARDS INCLUDE: 2001 Linbury Biennial Prize for Stage Design.

Max is an Associate Artist at Theatre Clwyd.

AISLING LOFTUS (Leonie Fowler)

THEATRE INCLUDES: We Happy Few (Nottingham Arts Theatre)

FOR NATIONAL THEATRE CONNECTIONS: He's Talking, The Spider Men, Just, The Musicians (National/Castle Theatre, Wellingborough/Nottingham Playhouse).

TELEVISION INCLUDES: Sleepyhead, Five Daughters, The Fattest Man in Britain, Dive, Doctors, Casualty, The Bill, The Worst Witch, Peak Practice.

FILM INCLUDES: Oranges and Sunshine, Summer, Blind Man's Alley, This Is England, Outlaw. Shorts: Jade, Ripe.

JORDAN LOUGHRAN (Emma M)

TELEVISION INCLUDES: UGetMe, Saving Nellie, (presenter) Richmond English 24.

RADIO: Lamplighters.

JAMES McARDLE (Daniel Mast)

THEATRE INCLUDES: Macbeth (Shakespeare's Globe); A Month in the Country (Chichester Festival Theatre).

TELEVISION INCLUDES: Stacey Stone, Recycled, Neverland.

FILM INCLUDES: Strictly Sinatra.

YASMIN PAIGE (Emma G)

THEATRE INCLUDES: Les Miserables (West End); Romeo & Juliet (Bloomsbury Theatre).

TELEVISION INCLUDES: Murderland, The Sarah Jane Adventures, Ballet Shoes, Secret Life, My Life as a Popat, Golden Hour, The Mysti Show, The Last Detective, Doctors, Keen Eddie.

FILM INCLUDES: True True Lie, I Could Never Be Your Woman, The Keeper, Tooth.

AWARDS INCLUDE: 2004 Annual Children's Entertainment Best Actress Award for Tooth.

MALCOLM RIPPETH (Lighting Designer)

THEATRE INCLUDES: Brief Encounter (Kneehigh Theatre/West End/ UK & US tours); Six Characters in Search of an Author, Calendar Girls (Chichester/West End/UK & Australian tours); The Devil Inside Him (National Theatre Wales); Don John, Cymbeline, Nights at the Circus, The Bacchae (Kneehigh); The Winslow Boy (also tour), Dumb Show (Rose, Kingston); Dark Side of Buffoon (Coventry/Lyric Hammersmith); His Dark Materials (Birmingham Rep/tour); Edward Gant's Amazing Feats of Loneliness, Faustus (Headlong); The Grouch, The Lion the Witch and the Wardrobe, Homage to Catalonia (West Yorkshire Playhouse); Mother Courage, Hamlet (English Touring Theatre); James and the Giant Peach (Northampton Royal); The Bloody Chamber, The Little Prince (Northern Stage); Trance (Bush); Confessions of a Justified Sinner, Copenhagen (Edinburgh Royal Lyceum); Monkey! (Dundee Rep); Tutti Frutti (National Theatre of Scotland).

OPERA & DANCE INCLUDES: Armida, Le Nozze Di Figaro, The Philosophers' Stone (Garsington Opera); Carmen Jones (Royal Festival Hall); Seven Deadly Sins (WNO/Diversions Dance) and numerous productions for balletLORENT, most recently Designer Body and Blood, Sweat & Tears.

AWARDS INCLUDE: 2009 Theatregoers' Choice Award for Best Lighting Designer for Brief Encounter and Six Characters in Search of an Author and, as a member of the design team, won the 2010 OBIE Award for Brief Encounter in New York.

SHARON SMALL (Vicky Evans)

THEATRE INCLUDES: Life is a Dream, Threepenny Opera (Donmar); The Exonerated (Riverside Studios); Lear (Sheffield Crucible); When Harry Met Sally (West End); Green Fields (Traverse); Insignificance (Chichester Festival Theatre); The London Cuckolds (National); Armstrong's Last Goodnight, School For Wives, Travesties (Edinburgh Lyceum); The Nun (Greenwich Studio); Suddenly Last Summer, The Forsythe Saga (Horseshoe Theatre, Basingstoke/tour); Himself (Nuffield Theatre, Southampton/tour); Pinocchio (Unicorn); Little Shop of Horrors, Wuthering Heights (Perth Theatre); A Comedy of Errors, My Cousin Rachel, A Chorus of Disapproval (Mercury, Colchester); The Cherry Orchard, Separate Tables, Arsenic and Old Lace, The Circle (Pitlochry Festival Theatre); Speed the Plow, Sexual Perversity in Chicago (Cambridge); The Broken Jug (Edinburgh Festival).

TELEVISION INCLUDES: Marple, Murderland, Mistresses, Inspector Lynley Mysteries, Midsummer Night's Dream, Cutting It, Glasgow Kiss, Sunburn, No Child of Mine, Hamish Macbeth, The Bill, Dr Finlay, An Independent Man, Roughnecks, Taggart.

FILM INCLUDES: Last Chance Harvey, Dear Frankie, About a Boy, Bumping the Odds, Bite, Driven, Pop Art.

MONIQUE STERLING (Assistant Director)

THEATRE INCLUDES: In the Solitude of Cotton Fields (The Clare, Young Vic); A Certain Child (Michael Frayn Studio); Mystical Awakening Extravaganza (BAC); Tuesday (Soho Studio); Ache (Baron's Court Theatre); Dinner Party (George Wood Theatre).

AS ASSISTANT DIRECTOR: Young NHS project (The Clare, Young Vic); Troilus and Cressida (Shakespeare's Globe); Tunnel 228 (Punchdrunk/Old Vic/Young Vic); Betting on the Dust Commander (Albany Theatre); The Worth of Thunder (Soho Studio); 2008 Schools Festival (Young Vic).

Monique is Trainee Director at the Royal Court, supported by the BBC writersroom.

SHANNON TARBET (Delilah Evans)

Shannon is making her professional debut in Spur of the Moment.

JERWOOD
NEW PLAYWRIGHTS

Since 1994 Jerwood New Playwrights has contributed to 67 new plays at the Royal Court including Joe Penhall's SOME VOICES, Mark Ravenhill's SHOPPING AND FUCKING (co-production with Out of Joint), Ayub Khan Din's EAST IS EAST (co-production with Tamasha), Martin McDonagh's THE BEAUTY QUEEN OF LEENANE (co-production with Druid Theatre Company), Conor McPherson's THE WEIR, Nick Grosso's REAL CLASSY AFFAIR, Sarah Kane's 4.48 PSYCHOSIS, Gary Mitchell's THE FORCE OF CHANGE, David Eldridge's UNDER THE BLUE SKY, David Harrower's PRESENCE, Simon Stephens' HERONS, Roy Williams' CLUBLAND, Leo Butler's REDUNDANT, Michael Wynne's THE PEOPLE ARE FRIENDLY, David Greig's OUTLYING ISLANDS, Zinnie Harris' NIGHTINGALE AND CHASE, Grae Cleugh's FUCKING GAMES, Rona Munro's IRON, Richard Bean's UNDER THE WHALEBACK, Ché Walker's FLESH WOUND, Roy Williams' FALLOUT, Mick Mahoney's FOOD CHAIN, Ayub Khan Din's NOTES ON FALLING LEAVES, Leo Butler's LUCKY DOG, Simon Stephens' COUNTRY MUSIC, Laura Wade's BREATHING CORPSES, Debbie Tucker Green's STONING MARY, David Eldridge's INCOMPLETE AND RANDOM ACTS OF KINDNESS, Gregory Burke's ON TOUR, Stella Feehily's O GO MY MAN, Simon Stephens' MOTORTOWN, Simon Farquhar's RAINBOW KISS, April de Angelis, Stella Feehily, Tanika Gupta, Chloe Moss and Laura Wade's CATCH, Mike Bartlett's MY CHILD, Polly Stenham's THAT FACE, Alexi Kaye Campbell's THE PRIDE, Fiona Evans' SCARBOROUGH, Levi David Addai's OXFORD STREET and Bola Agbaje's GONE TOO FAR!.

Last year Jerwood New Playwrights supported Alia Bano's SHADES, Polly Stenham's TUSK TUSK and Tim Crouch's THE AUTHOR. So far in 2010, Jerwood New Playwrights has supported Bola Agbaje's OFF THE ENDZ and DC Moore's THE EMPIRE. Jerwood New Playwrights is supported by the Jerwood Charitable Foundation.

The Jerwood Charitable Foundation is committed to imaginative and responsible revenue funding of the arts, supporting artists at important stages in their development and across all art forms. www.jerwoodcharitablefoundation.org

DC Moore's THE EMPIRE
(photo: Nobby Clark)

Tim Crouch's THE AUTHOR
(photo: Steve Cummiskey)

THE ENGLISH STAGE COMPANY
AT THE ROYAL COURT THEATRE

'For me the theatre is really a religion or way of life. You must decide what you feel the world is about and what you want to say about it, so that everything in the theatre you work in is saying the same thing ... A theatre must have a recognisable attitude. It will have one, whether you like it or not.'

George Devine, first artistic director of the English Stage Company: notes for an unwritten book.

photo: Stephen Cummiskey

As Britain's leading national company dedicated to new work, the Royal Court Theatre produces new plays of the highest quality, working with writers from all backgrounds, and addressing the problems and possibilities of our time.

"The Royal Court has been at the centre of British cultural life for the past 50 years, an engine room for new writing and constantly transforming the theatrical culture." Stephen Daldry

Since its foundation in 1956, the Royal Court has presented premieres by almost every leading contemporary British playwright, from John Osborne's Look Back in Anger to Caryl Churchill's A Number and Tom Stoppard's Rock 'n' Roll. Just some of the other writers to have chosen the Royal Court to premiere their work include Edward Albee, John Arden, Richard Bean, Samuel Beckett, Edward Bond, Leo Butler, Jez Butterworth, Martin Crimp, Ariel Dorfman, Stella Feehily, Christopher Hampton, David Hare, Eugène Ionesco, Ann Jellicoe, Terry Johnson, Sarah Kane, David Mamet, Martin McDonagh, Conor McPherson, Joe Penhall, Lucy Prebble, Mark Ravenhill, Simon Stephens, Wole Soyinka, Polly Stenham, David Storey, Debbie Tucker Green, Arnold Wesker and Roy Williams.

"It is risky to miss a production there." Financial Times

In addition to its full-scale productions, the Royal Court also facilitates international work at a grass roots level, developing exchanges which bring young writers to Britain and sending British writers, actors and directors to work with artists around the world. The research and play development arm of the Royal Court Theatre, The Studio, finds the most exciting and diverse range of new voices in the UK. The Studio runs play-writing groups including the Young Writers Programme, Critical Mass for black, Asian and minority ethnic writers and the biennial Young Writers Festival. For further information, go to www.royalcourttheatre.com/ywp.

"Yes, the Royal Court is on a roll. Yes, Dominic Cooke has just the genius and kick that this venue needs... It's fist-bitingly exciting." Independent

PROGRAMME SUPPORTERS

The Royal Court (English Stage Company Ltd) receives its principal funding from Arts Council England, London. It is also supported financially by a wide range of private companies, charitable and public bodies, and earns the remainder of its income from the box office and its own trading activities.

The Genesis Foundation supports the Royal Court's work with International Playwrights. Theatre Local is sponsored by Bloomberg. The Jerwood Charitable Foundation supports new plays by new playwrights through the Jerwood New Playwrights series. £10 Monday Nights is sponsored by French Wines: Wines of Quality.

The Artistic Director's Chair is supported by a lead grant from The Peter Jay Sharp Foundation, contributing to the activities of the Artistic Director's office. Over the past ten years the BBC has supported the Gerald Chapman Fund for directors.

FOR THE ROYAL COURT

Royal Court Theatre, Sloane Square, London SW1W 8AS
Tel: 020 7565 5050 Fax: 020 7565 5001
info@royalcourttheatre.com, www.royalcourttheatre.com

Artistic Director **Dominic Cooke**
Deputy Artistic Director **Jeremy Herrin**
Associate Director **Sacha Wares***
Artistic Associate **Emily McLaughlin***
Diversity Associate **Ola Animashawun***
Education Associate **Lynne Gagliano***
Producer **Vanessa Stone***
Trainee Director **Monique Sterling**‡

Literary Manager **Christopher Campbell**
Senior Reader **Nicola Wass****
Literary Assistant **Marcelo Dos Santos**
Studio Administrator **Clare McQuillan**
Writers' Tutor **Leo Butler***
Pearson Playwright (The John Mortimer Award)
Alia Bano

Associate Director International **Elyse Dodgson**
International Projects Manager **Chris James**
International Assistant **William Drew**

Casting Director (Maternity Cover) **Julia Horan**
Casting Director **Amy Ball**
Casting Assistant **Lotte Hines**

Head of Production **Paul Handley**
JTU Production Manager **Tariq Rifaat**
Production Administrator **Sarah Davies**
Head of Lighting **Matt Drury**
Lighting Deputy **Stephen Andrews**
Lighting Assistants **Katie Pitt, Jack Williams**
Head of Stage **Steven Stickler**
Stage Deputy **Duncan Russell**
Stage Chargehand **Lee Crimmen**
Chargehand Carpenter **Richard Martin**
Head of Sound **David McSeveney**
Sound Deputy **Alex Caplen**
Sound Operator **Helen Skiera**
Head of Costume **Iona Kenrick**
Costume Deputy **Jackie Orton**
Wardrobe Assistant **Pam Anson**

Executive Director **Kate Horton**
Head of Finance & Administration **Helen Perryer**
Planning Administrator **Davina Shah**
Production Assistant **David Nock**
Senior Finance & Administration Officer **Martin Wheeler**
Finance Officer **Rachel Harrison***
Finance & Administration Assistant **Tessa Rivers**
PA to the Executive Director **Caroline Morris**

Head of Communications **Kym Bartlett**
Marketing Manager **Becky Wootton**
Press & Public Relations Officer **Anna Evans**
Communications Assistant **Ruth Hawkins**
Communications Interns **Philippa Crossman**
Sales Manager **Kevin West**
Deputy Sales Manager **Daniel Alicandro**
Box Office Sales Assistants **Cheryl Gallagher, Ciara O'Toole, Helen Murray***, **Natalie Tarjanyi***, **Amanda Wilkin***

Head of Development **Gaby Styles**
Senior Development Manager **Hannah Clifford**
Trusts & Foundations Manager **Khalila Hassouna**
Development Officer **Lucy Buxton**
Development Assistant **Penny Saward**
US Fundraising Counsel **Tim Runion**

Theatre Manager **Bobbie Stokes**
Deputy Theatre Manager **Daniel O'Neill**
Duty Managers **Fiona Clift***, **Claire Simpson***
Events Manager **Joanna Ostrom**
Deputy Bar & Food Manager **Sami Rifaat**
Bar & Food Supervisor **Ali Christian**
Bar & Food Duty Supervisor **Becca Walton**
Head Chef **Charlie Brookman**
Bookshop Manager **Simon David**
Assistant Bookshop Manager **Edin Suljic***
Bookshop Assistant **Vanessa Hammick** *
Customer Service Assistant **Deirdre Lennon***
Stage Door/Reception **Simon David***, **Paul Lovegrove, Tyrone Lucas**

Thanks to all of our box office assistants, ushers and bar staff.

** The post of Senior Reader is supported by NoraLee & Jon Sedmak through the American Friends of the Royal Court Theatre.

‡ The post of the Trainee Director is supported by the BBC writersroom.

* Part-time.

ENGLISH STAGE COMPANY

President
Dame Joan Plowright CBE

Honorary Council
Sir Richard Eyre CBE
Alan Grieve CBE
Martin Paisner CBE

Council
Chairman **Anthony Burton**
Vice Chairman **Graham Devlin CBE**

Members
Jennette Arnold
Judy Daish
Sir David Green KCMG
Joyce Hytner OBE
Stephen Jeffreys
Wasfi Kani OBE
Phyllida Lloyd CBE
James Midgley
Sophie Okonedo OBE
Alan Rickman
Anita Scott
Katharine Viner
Stewart Wood

SPUR OF THE MOMENT

Anya Reiss

SPUR OF THE MOMENT

OBERON BOOKS
LONDON

First published in 2010 by Oberon Books Ltd
521 Caledonian Road, London N7 9RH
Tel: +44 (0) 20 7607 3637 / Fax: +44 (0) 20 7607 3629
e-mail: info@oberonbooks.com
www.oberonbooks.com

Reprinted in 2010, 2011

A catalogue record for this book is available from the British
Library.

ISBN: 978-1-84002-985-7

Cover image by Adam Gault

Printed in Great Britain by Marston Book Services Ltd., Didcot.

Characters

DELILAH EVANS, (Almost) 13

DANIEL MAST, 21

VICKY EVANS, 45

NICK EVANS, 52

LEONIE FOWLER, 19

EMMA G, 12

NAOMI, 13

EMMA M, 13

SETTING

Daniel's bed is the most important piece of furniture on the set. To me the Evans house is a detached house in Surrey, the action never leaves the house

Delilah's bedroom

The kitchen

Daniel's bedroom

Living room

Hallway outside Daniel's bedroom

Sometimes actions happen in hallways just outside rooms

'There are two tragedies in life. One is to lose your heart's desire. The other is to gain it'

George Bernard Shaw

ACT ONE

SCENE ONE

Friday 5pm. Darkness, a few seconds pass with nothing then 'Now or Never' from High School Musical 3 begins playing into the darkness. The first two lines pass then with 'game on' DELILAH EVANS, EMMA M, EMMA G and NAOMI are all revealed sitting on the floor in Delilah's bedroom. A phone is in the centre of the group and a CD player behind them. Emma G bored whereas the others are apparently waiting for something in the music.

DELILAH: Okay get ready, get ready

NAOMI: Shut up!

EMMA M: Hang on they do it again

NAOMI: *(Counts the others in then...)* Now! Now! Now!

> *EMMA G presses record on the phone, everyone except her starts singing.*

EMMA M, NAOMI, and DELILAH: *(Sing the first few lines of the first verse of 'Now or Never'.)*

EMMA G: *(About the phone.)* Wait, wait it's stopped

NAOMI: Why?

EMMA M: What?

NAOMI: Put it on pause

> *DELILAH leans over and pauses the music, they crowd round the phone.*

EMMA G: Only records for a little bit

EMMA M: That's shit

DELILAH: How do you make it playback?

EMMA G: Can we please leave it now?

NAOMI: Let's use mine *(Puts her phone in the middle.)*

EMMA G: Oh my god you got it!

DELILAH: What?

NAOMI: New blackberry

DELILAH: Really? (The Storm)?

EMMA M: Not now, can we please do the chorus?

DELILAH: Okay *(Starts fast forwarding the music.)*

EMMA G: Oh my days! Can we stop? Please

NAOMI: Do it with us

EMMA G: *(With disgust.)* I've never seen High School Musical!

EMMA M: Look at her face

EMMA G: Or like Justin Bieber or Witches of Waverly Place or Hannah Mon-fucking-tana

DELILAH: Okay, okay get ready

The music starts again, they count themselves, singing parts as they wait for the chorus, EMMA G presses record.

EMMA M, DELILAH, NAOMI: *(Sing chorus of 'Now or Never'.)*

EMMA M: Stop!

The phone is stopped, they crowd round it excited, someone turns off or down the music.

EMMA G: Do you have to listen to it back?

NAOMI: Sh!

They listen to their recording.

EMMA M: It's so cool!

NAOMI: That's going to be my ringtone

EMMA M: Send it to me. Go on Bluetooth

EMMA G: Please do that later

EMMA M: Two seconds, God!

EMMA G: *(Changing subject.)* Delilah what's happening Sunday then?

DELILAH: Come over here first then watch Harry Potter DVDs

NAOMI and EMMA M together: *(In a special voice they always use.)* Harry Potter!

NAOMI: Harry and Ginny!

EMMA M: What was the last film?

NAOMI: Harry and Ginny

EMMA M: I can't remember what happens

DELILAH: Harry and Ginny get...

NAOMI: Basically Harry finds the potions book by the Half Blood Prince...

EMMA M: Who is the Prince again?

NAOMI: Snape! And Harry and Ginny get together and Ron and Lavender get together and Hermione is sad then there is all the Horcrux stuff and Dumbledore dies

EMMA M: Oh yeah

NAOMI: Oh my God have you seen the new trailer, was on MTV?

EMMA M: No

DELILAH: For Deathly Hallows, was amazing

NAOMI: You've got to see it Emma was so good

DELILAH: With Voldermort

NAOMI: 'I must be the one to kill Harry Potter'

DELILAH: With the train

NAOMI: With the hand

EMMA M: Have you found me yet?

NAOMI: *(About phone.)* Are you Princess Cool 125?

EMMA M: No

NAOMI: Okay we're coming here then what?

DELILAH: Um then we'll...

EMMA M: *(Interfering.)* We'll have pizza and we're...

NAOMI: Are you going to bring cake into school on Monday?

EMMA M: Bring in Colin the Caterpillar Cake

NAOMI: Shotgun the head!

EMMA M: Shotgun the bum!

DELILAH: Ok

EMMA M: *(Talking about the phone again.)* That's me

NAOMI: It's transferring

There is a creak outside and someone walks past DELILAH's room.

EMMA G: I thought your mum was out

DELILAH: It's only Daniel

NAOMI: He's so hot!

DELILAH: Sh he'll hear you!

NAOMI: *(Pretending to call.)* You're so hot

DELILAH: Shut up!

EMMA M: I don't think he's hot

NAOMI: Have you ever met him?

EMMA M: You showed me him on Facebook

DELILAH: You have him on Facebook?

NAOMI: Yeah

DELILAH: He accepted you?

NAOMI: That photo of him on holiday with that girl!

DELILAH: Leonie

NAOMI: So hot! Delilah get him to come in here

DELILAH: No

EMMA G: Are your parents coming on Sunday?

DELILAH: Well they'll be here

EMMA G: I thought we were going swimming after

DELILAH: Yeah my mum'll come

EMMA G: Can't he come instead?

DELILAH: Daniel?

EMMA M: Is he nice?

DELILAH: Yeah really nice

NAOMI: You want to... *(Singing 'Fuck Forever' by Babyshambles.)*

DELILAH: No I don't shut up

EMMA M: That song is so old

NAOMI: I love Babyshambles right now

EMMA M: I swear they're like dead

NAOMI: No

EMMA M: Well I haven't heard anything about them for ages

NAOMI: No Pete Doherty is just...

EMMA M: Whatever Naomi, will you ask Daniel?

DELILAH: Why would he come?

NAOMI: He's looking after us now isn't he?

DELILAH: Yeah, so?

NAOMI: So can't he be like our chaperone instead of your mum?

DELILAH: He's just like keeping an eye on us now it's different if I ask him to come out

EMMA G: Your mum could pay him

EMMA M: Your mum paid him last night

EMMA G: Your mum tipped him last night *(They laugh.)*

DELILAH: My mum won't pay him! He won't come; I mean like your brother Emma wouldn't chaperone you on your bir...

NAOMI: But he's not your brother he's just the lodger

EMMA G: The fucking hot lodger

DANIEL MAST walks past the room again, they go silent then all laugh except Delilah.

DELILAH: Oh my god I bet he heard you!

NAOMI: That's so embarrassing!

EMMA G: I can never come round again

NAOMI: Delilah can you please just ask him?

EMMA M: I thought you were friends with him

NAOMI: No she just likes him

DELILAH: No!

NAOMI: You said he was nice

DELILAH: Yeah and we're friends

NAOMI: No you're not!

DELILAH: What?

NAOMI: I mean you don't like hang out together

DELILAH: Yeah we do

NAOMI: You don't understand what I mean

DELILAH: He won't want to hang out with a whole load of 13 year olds

DANIEL comes back, they go silent, he knocks on the door and puts his head into the room, the others are surprised as it seems she wasn't lying about being friends.

DANIEL: Everything alright Del'?

DELILAH: Yeah

DANIEL: Just checking

DELILAH: *(Playfully.)* Well go check somewhere else

DANIEL: *(To her friends.)* Got a gob on her this one hasn't she?

DELILAH: Just like you!

DANIEL: Shut your face

DELILAH: Shut *your* face

DANIEL: That's rather rude, just checking you're alright, that you're not running a harem....

DELILAH: Get out

DANIEL: You'll miss me

DELILAH: Go, go *(Throws something at him.)*

DANIEL: *(Catches object.)* Cheers love, see you girls

DANIEL leaves, slight pause.

EMMA G: He's so hot!

EMMA M: You should have asked him then

NAOMI's phone beeps.

NAOMI: It's transferred

EMMA M: Shall we do the next bit with Troy?

EMMA G: No please I fucking beg you!

EMMA M: I'm Gabrielle, you're Troy, Emma you're Chad

EMMA G: No!

NAOMI: Okay no one's Chad, Delilah find the bit where she stands up. Shall we film it?

EMMA M: Yeah okay

EMMA G: Do I have to?

NAOMI: Okay get ready

The music plays.

NAOMI: Okay now

EMMA M: Record

They sing loudly and with exaggerated actions, they work much better than when DELILAH was with them. They take the parts of the characters in the film, in synch with each other and the music – they've done this before. They sing Troy and Garbrielle's verse from 'High School Musical'. They start jumping round and move back to do the cheerleaders dance. EMMA G passing DELILAH the camera who continues filming.

In the kitchen, High School Musical continues playing from DELILAH's bedroom, NICK EVANS and VICKY EVANS enter, dressed smartly.

NICK: Do you think Delilah is back?

VICKY: Yes, can't you hear her music?

NICK: Do you want me to get her to turn it down?

VICKY sits at the kitchen table, eases off her heels.

VICKY: No it's fine

NICK: This is from that film, isn't it?

VICKY: Hm?

NICK: That film with all the kids in it

VICKY: Oh yes, yes, think it is

NICK: You okay?

VICKY: Yes

NICK: He had a horrible suit didn't...

VICKY: Yes he did

NICK: Really tacky you think he'd...

VICKY: Yes you would

NICK: You would

Music finishes.

NICK: That's better, do you want a cup of tea?

VICKY: No I'm fine

NICK: Sure?

VICKY: Yes

NICK: Coffee?

VICKY: Only if it's real

NICK: I'll make it real *(Pause as he wonders whether to say it or not.)* would have been easier to just say

VICKY: Say what?

NICK: Say you wanted coffee

VICKY: I just did

NICK: At the start rather than me having to guess

VICKY: Don't start Nick already, we've just come in...

NICK: I'm not starting, darling

VICKY: What have I done then?

NICK: It's not a big deal! All I mean is; I offered you tea, you could have said 'no but I would like a cup of real coffee please' rather than me having to offer a thousand and one things to you trying to guess what it is you want

VICKY: You didn't have to

NICK: I did, else you would say later 'we came in and you didn't even offer me a drink'

VICKY: Well you would have, you would have offered me a drink, tea, which I refused

NICK: I know and when I would point that out to you, you would have said 'yes but I only drink coffee, don't I Nick, you know I don't drink tea'

VICKY: Well you do know that but you still offered tea!

27

NICK: Vicky this is ridiculous!

VICKY: Yes it is fucking ridiculous that you always say tea even though I've never drunk it

NICK: Last week at Delilah's parents evening *(VICKY groans.)* they offered you tea and...

VICKY: Oh don't start that again we know full well I drunk tea then because you went ballistic

NICK: Then why say you've never drunk tea in your life when we've even argued over you drinking tea

VICKY: Then offering me tea was just fucking stupid, wasn't it?

NICK: Well I wasn't thinking

VICKY: Ob-vi-ous-ly!

NICK: Well you ob-vi-ous-ly drink tea now, don't you?

VICKY: What?

NICK: Because of Delilah's parents evening

VICKY: For God's sake, can we leave it?

NICK: No Vicky because you're starting at me yet again, yet a-fucking-gain

VICKY: For God's sake Nick! Her teacher offered me tea and I hadn't drunk anything all day so when you acted like I was your pathetic little wife by saying 'oh my wife doesn't drink tea' I did get annoyed and accepted, I didn't know me contradicting you would be such a fucking blow to your manhood. I promise now like I did last week that I will never, ever, ever accept any drink from anyone ever again because...

NICK: You're just being completely over dramatic

VICKY: Will you let me fucking finish what I'm saying?

NICK: No because you're talking rubbish

VICKY: Let me finish!

NICK: For God's sake!

VICKY: Nick! Let me finish what I was going to say

NICK: Go on then

VICKY: What?

NICK: Go on then

VICKY: What?

NICK: Say what you want to say!

VICKY: I...I can't even fucking remember! *(NICK laughs triumphantly.)* If you hadn't interrupted me I wouldn't have forgotten

NICK: So it's my fault?

VICKY: Yes

NICK: All my fault?

VICKY: Yes, Nick wallow you self indulgent wanker. Yes you are the victim of the world...

NICK: Everything in the world is my fault. You forget what you are saying – my fault. Blame me for everything...

VICKY: Yes I do I do blame you for everything Nick. I can't fucking stand you

NICK: Well I can't fucking stand you

VICKY: We can't go on like this

NICK: Here we go with the over dramatics Vicky. Why not start crying? Why not get hysterical? Why not paint the fucking house in your blood to prove how much you suffer!

VICKY: Shut up Nick!

NICK: Shut up Vicky!

VICKY: You're such a child

NICK: That's right scream the house down why not get Daniel and Delilah and all her friends down to watch what an evil man I am

VICKY: And you call me overdramatic!

NICK: You are

VICKY: Can't you just be nice to me for one day? Today has been really hard for me...

NICK: I've had enough of hearing how tough it is for you I'm not having the best time either

VICKY: That's right all about you

NICK: All about me! What? What! It's always about you...

VICKY: Right now it should be, it's your fault we're in this mess

NICK: I've said I'm sorry day and fucking night. I'm not breathing anymore I just murmur sorry, I snore sorry, I eat fucking humble pie and choke on lumps of sorry, I shit sorry. Vicky sorry! Sorry! Sorry!

VICKY: Oh it's good to know you mean it, oh the waves of comfort overwhelm me. Oh wait my mistake it's a fucking tsunami!

NICK: It was the worst thing I've ever done in my life, I shouldn't have done it, it was...I'm sorry Vicky it was spur of the moment...

VICKY: Spur of the moment it went on for weeks Nick! I can't take this any....

NICK: Get over it Vicky!

VICKY: Get over it!

NICK: You said you needed time, you've fucking had it. Christ let it go

VICKY: Oh yes, okay, you're right Nick, I've let it go, bye bye feelings

NICK: Sarcasm is the lowest form of wit

VICKY: And you are the lowest form of life Nick

NICK: *(Claps.)* Oh well done Vicky well done

VICKY: That's sarcastic you hypocritical bastard

NICK: That's not sarcastic that's ironic

VICKY: My God!

NICK: Look talking calmly and reasonably...

VICKY: Fuck off Nick

NICK: Today was hard but not just for you

VICKY: It's your fault though

NICK: Okay I know. I know

VICKY: So why should I feel sorry for you?

NICK: I'm not asking you to feel...

VICKY: Why would I be sympathetic for a cheating broke lying piece of shit!

NICK: Go on

VICKY: A stupid little idiot who can't control himself...

NICK: Keep it coming

VICKY: The total embarrassment of a pathetic individual who crawled out of bed...

NICK: Go on drag it all up again

VICKY: Fucked their boss for five months!

NICK: Four

VICKY: What?

NICK: Four months, I fucked her for *(He stops, slight pause.)*

VICKY: Oh well that's okay then if it was only four

NICK: I didn't mean that

31

VICKY: And then you lost your job

NICK: I didn't lose...

VICKY: Contract not renewed then Nick it adds up to the same thing

NICK: It's wasn't because of...

VICKY: Yes of course of course

NICK: I said! I said do you want me to do something about this get a lawyer...

VICKY: Three months later you said! Three months later you explained

NICK: That doesn't matter, that doesn't matter, you said no

VICKY: I'm sorry Nick I was saving for a billboard for outside the damn house saying Nick Evans cheated on his fucking wife

NICK: You know the worst thing about all this, the very worst thing

VICKY: Oh there's worse?

NICK: Yes there's worse

VICKY: Worse than losing your job cause you're such an idiot as to fuck your own boss, worse than cheating on your wife for an older and uglier model, worse than all the embarrassment you've caused, worse than us having to have a lodger, worse than us having to go to the bank today and remortgage our own house because of your selfish stupidity, worse than...

NICK: Yes, yes worse than all of that!

VICKY: Worse? Go on then, go on

NICK: The worst thing about all of this...

VICKY: Go on I'm waiting, tell me

NICK: I am fucking telling you

VICKY: Get on with it then!

NICK: The worst thing...

VICKY: Stop starting from the beginning all over again just say it rather than this fucking introduction

NICK: The worst thing...

VICKY: Nick why don't you ever listen?

NICK: The worst thing is that you think that this is all so dramatic and amazing and it makes you so wonderfully wronged and beautiful and you belong in some shitty film when actually it just makes you sad, pathetic, ugly and boring

VICKY: *(Sarcastic.)* Oh that hurts so much, cuts right to the bone

NICK: And the worst thing is that you think this is new when actually this kind of thing has happened to thousands of women for hundreds and thousands of years and they all react and look and sound like you. So actually it hasn't even made you special!

VICKY: Oh shut up Nick

NICK: You fucking shut up!

VICKY: Shut up Nick!

VICKY throws a mug, it smashes on the floor unnoticed by both.

NICK: Shut up Vi...

VICKY: *(Completely losing it.)* Shut up! Shut up! Shut up!

She finally sits and cries, NICK stands over her embarrassed and fuming.

NICK: All over a fucking cup of fucking tea

NAOMI pushes EMMA M into the room then follows herself aware that they've walked in on an argument, giggling.

NAOMI: Mr Evans is it okay if we... *(Starts laughing.)*

33

EMMA M: Have some pepperoni sticks?

NICK: What?

EMMA M: Can we please get some pepperoni sticks from the fridge?

NICK: Yes

NAOMI: Thank you Mr Evans

They go to the fridge still laughing. EMMA whispers something to NAOMI, they tussle at the fridge, NAOMI persuaded into doing something, nudged, she turns

NAOMI: Is everything alright Mrs Evans?

Pause, they start giggling.

NICK: Vicky

VICKY: What?

NICK: Vicky *(Indicates the girls.)*

VICKY: Yes absolutely fine in fact it's absolutely wonderful. Would you like me to fix you girls some snacks and drinks?

NAOMI: Um...

EMMA M: It's okay we're going now

VICKY: Oh okay girls and send my love to your mum Diana

The girls look at each other and laugh.

NAOMI: I'm Naomi

VICKY: I know

EMMA M: Um Mrs Evans it's me Emma

VICKY: I know your names

NICK: *(Warning.)* Vicky

The girls laugh again.

NAOMI: Um we're just going upstairs...

VICKY: Okay play nicely Diana

The girls run upstairs laughing.

NICK: For fuck's sake

VICKY: What? Stupid little brats if we're not careful Delilah will turn out to be just like them

NICK: Do you want to be the laughing stock of the county?

VICKY: Not particularly but what choice have I got?

NICK goes to argue but VICKY picks up her heels and leaves the room.

SCENE TWO

Friday 7pm. DELILAH lies on DANIEL's bed playing with her feet, he is at a laptop. DANIEL answers without looking up from the screen.

DELILAH: Would you rather be Batman or Spiderman?

DANIEL: Spiderman

DELILAH: Spiderman's gay!

DANIEL: Batman's got no special powers and is always miserable

DELILAH: Give me three reasons to be Spiderman not Batman

DANIEL: One Batman is miserable, two Spiderman can sling webs and three Spiderman fucks Kirsten Dunst

DELILAH: Three reasons to be Batman not Spiderman; number one Spiderman is a reporter in his spare time, Batman is a billionaire

DANIEL: Touché

DELILAH: What's that mean?

DANIEL: Never mind

DELILAH: Two Batman is hot and three can fuck anyone he likes. I've got the DVD somewhere

DANIEL: Which one?

DELILAH: Dark Knight. It's one of those Italian illegal DVD's I've got, do you want to see it?

DANIEL: You can put them on English right?

DELILAH: Ob-vi-ous-ly

DANIEL: Then ob-vi-ous-ly I'll watch it

DELILAH: We can watch it tonight then okay?

DANIEL: Okay

DELILAH: Okay *(Pause then draws out the word.)* Daniel...

DANIEL: Wha...? *(Sees she is teasing him, tries to concentrate on computer.)*

DELILAH: Danny...Dan *(Sings his name to Batman theme tune.)* Danny, Danny, Danny, Danny, Danny, Danny, Danny, Danny, Dan-man, Dan-man, Dan-man, Danny, Danny...

DANIEL: *(Gets up and comes over to the bed.)* What? What you annoying little buzzing moronic child?

DELILAH: I'm cold

DANIEL: Your dad never turns the heating on

DELILAH rolls over in the duvet pulling it with her so she is wrapped up in it.

DELILAH: 'Cause he is a mean bastard

DANIEL: Get out of there you'll mess it up *(Pushing her around in the bed.)*

DELILAH: Huh worse than before?

DANIEL: Yeah worse than before you cheeky bitch *(DELILAH starts examining his arm.)*

DELILAH: He buys economy things in Tesco

DANIEL: Who?

DELILAH: My dad

DANIEL: You're so harsh on him *(Sits on bed next to her.)*

DELILAH: I'm not harsh. You've got white marks across your arm

DANIEL: I heard you begging for a Blackberry Storm earlier

DELILAH: Naomi has one; everyone has one I want to BBM people

DANIEL: He can't afford it

DELILAH: Shut up he's still fuck rich

Pause.

DELILAH: Do you know what Daniel means?

DANIEL: No

DELILAH: God is my judge

DANIEL: Eurgh

DELILAH: Delilah means seductive

DANIEL laughs and she rolls out of duvet and settles herself across his lap.

DELILAH: *(Jokingly, like an imperial command.)* Sing to me Daniel

DANIEL: What?

DELILAH: The national anthem

DANIEL: The real one?

DELILAH: No my one

DANIEL: Fuck off

DELILAH: Daniel please

DANIEL: Delilah I'm busy

DELILAH: Daniel!

DANIEL: *(Sings guitar intro to 'Hey There Delilah' by the Plain White Ts.)*

DELILAH: *(Sings the first two phrases of the song over his humming.)*

The two sing together for a moment then as DANIEL forgets the words they reach the chorus and sing together for a line or two but the laptop makes the shutting down sound and DANIEL jumps up and goes to it.

DANIEL: Fuck, fuck, I didn't save! *(DELILAH doesn't move.)* Later Delilah

She goes to leave but DELILAH bumps into VICKY at the door.

VICKY: Sorry darling, I just wanted to ask you Daniel about Leonie

DANIEL: Oh yeah

DELILAH: When she coming?

DELILAH sits back on his bed, VICKY perches on the edge.

DANIEL: I was going to go and pick her up from the station at nine thirty

VICKY: Okay, and um... *(Embarrassed.)* would you introduce us all

DANIEL: Yes of course

VICKY: I'm sorry just I wouldn't, I don't know, want to bump into her on the stairs and...

DANIEL: No I understand, you want to know who's in your house

VICKY: *(Relieved.)* Yes, and she'll be in here?

NICK appears at the door.

NICK: Daniel I just wanted a word...oh this is where my family is

DANIEL: Yeah sorry I've collected them

DELILAH: Like stamps

NICK: *(Confused.)* What?

VICKY: Nick do knock before you come into his room you can't just burst in

NICK: I heard voices

VICKY: Even more reason not to burst in

DANIEL: Don't worry about it

NICK: *(Joking.)* I was breaking down the door to ensure you weren't having it off with my wife Daniel

DANIEL: *(Going along with the joke.)* Oh yes very wise she's a fine looking lady

NICK: More likely to be the other way round, let me know if she bothers you Daniel

DANIEL: Oh I doubt that

NICK: Clawing at your door begging to be let in

DANIEL: No

NICK: Middle of the night

VICKY: Nick

NICK: *(Imitating her.)* 'Daniel Daniel let me in'

VICKY: Nick!

NICK: Can't blame her! I'm getting on, can't blame her for looking elsewhere, only natural

DANIEL: Well I assure you Nicholas if she knocks I'll send her straight back to you

NICK: Can't blame you, I cannot blame you

NICK and VICKY are staring at each other, daring the other one on.

VICKY: *(Flirting.)* Really Daniel? You'd send me back?

DANIEL: I was…I'm only joking

VICKY: Sure I couldn't slip in *(DANIEL laughs nervously.)* Delilah finds her way into this room often enough sure we couldn't have a little friendship too? Delilah what's your secret way into this room

39

DANIEL: Alright I ban all of you from my room then

DELILAH: Daniel!

VICKY: Come on Daniel we'll try it tonight. Nick gets me up with his snoring and I'll lie in bed and think of you in the next room and I'll 'scratch' at your door. Would you have the heart to send me back to *him*?

DANIEL: I think I just won't answer the door and avoid the whole dilemma

VICKY: Come on Daniel tonight's my last chance with Leonie coming

NICK: Oh no it'll be the perfect cover I'll think all the noises will be Leonie and Daniel...

DELILAH: What noises?

NICK: When actually it'll be Daniel and you

DANIEL: *(Uncomfortable, laughs.)* We'll have to put the radio on Vicky then

VICKY: We always do Daniel we always do...Nick what was it you wanted?

NICK: To check everything was okay about Leonie

VICKY: It's all okay, isn't it Daniel?

NICK: Good

VICKY: Right

Pause.

NICK: I'm going to go read the paper

DANIEL: Cheers Nick

NICK wants to leave but waits for VICKY, pause.

VICKY: Right I better leave you to it

DANIEL nods, pause, VICKY leaves rubbing the back of DANIEL's head as she goes, NICK follows outraged.

DELILAH: Sorry about my mum, they're well embarrassing

DANIEL: It's okay *(Smoothing down his hair.)*

DELILAH: Will Leonie like me?

DANIEL: Course she will, she's a lovely girl... and so are you. Ah my computer's fucked

DELILAH: *(Trying to do a somersault on his bed.)* I'll inform the Queen

DANIEL: Shut up *(DANIEL looks up.)* What you doing?

DELILAH: Nothing

DANIEL: You're crazy. You still cold?

DELILAH: Yeah

DANIEL: Put a jumper on then

DELILAH starts searching through his jumpers.

DELILAH: Can I wear this?

DANIEL: Alright

DELILAH: I love wearing men's clothes

DANIEL: I don't really like it on girls

DELILAH: Why?

DANIEL: Like showing off isn't it

DELILAH: Do you not want me to wear this then?

DANIEL: No you're different I mean girlfriends and stuff, I never let Leonie wear my stuff. It's possessive

DELILAH: Of what? *(Pulling on jumper.)*

DANIEL: It's like to prove they are with a man

DELILAH: That's a bit deep

DELILAH jumps up, leans over his chair to see computer.

DANIEL: Don't get your sticky fingers all over my keyboard

DELILAH: Sticky fingers, how old do you think I am? I'm gonna be thirteen on Sunday

DANIEL: Oh yeah, that's right

DELILAH: A teenager

DANIEL: I always forget how young you are

DELILAH: Thirteen! Thirteen is really old I'm a teenager

DANIEL: It's not old

DELILAH: I say my age to old ladies now and they are like 'ah bless' when it's thirteen they'll start looking suspicious

DANIEL: I don't think anyone says you are sweet now

DELILAH: They do

DANIEL: Bad lips *(Puts his finger over her lip.)* tell lies

DELILAH: *(DELILAH looks at his arm, he moves his hand away, pulls down his sleeve.)* Will you come to my birthday?

DANIEL: Yeah, I got you a present and everything

DELILAH: Really?

DANIEL: Yeah

DELILAH: I didn't mean that though

DANIEL: What did you mean?

DELILAH: My friends are coming over then we're going swimming, will you come?

DANIEL: To look after you?

DELILAH: Kind of

DANIEL: When is it?

DELILAH: Sunday

DANIEL: Leonie's here

DELILAH: So? Won't be very long

DANIEL: But Del she's...

DELILAH: It's my birthday

DANIEL: I'll think about it

DELILAH: Where's my present then?

DANIEL: You've got to wait

DELILAH: *Where* is it though?

DANIEL: In that drawer next to my bed

She gets up, DANIEL holds her around the middle.

DANIEL: Uh where are you going? I haven't wrapped it yet

DELILAH turns to face him, his arms still around her middle.

DELILAH: You've totally tempted me now

DANIEL: Well you're just going to have to be tempted

DELILAH suddenly turns and jumps on to the bed, she lands on her front and reaches for the drawer. DANIEL stands up and tries to stop her, he pins her to the bed.

DELILAH: Get off you're hurting me

DANIEL: Never

DELILAH: What's wrong with your arm?

DANIEL: What? *(Sitting up.)*

DELILAH: You got like scars all over it

DANIEL: Cat

DELILAH: What cat?

DANIEL: When I had this crazy cat and when I was like a toddler...

DELILAH: Baby Daniel!

DANIEL: I pissed it off and it like ripped up my arm

DELILAH: Aw

DANIEL: Sorry did you want it to be a war wound?

43

DELILAH: That'd be hot

DANIEL: Girls are weird

DELILAH: Huh?

DANIEL: If you were all scarred I wouldn't think...

DELILAH: Think what?

DANIEL: You've forgotten about your present then?

DELILAH: Oh yeah get off

DANIEL: Nope

DELILAH: I'll get my mum

DANIEL: And what will she do?

DELILAH: When she sees you mauling me?

DANIEL: Yeah

DELILAH: Probably join in *(They laugh embarrassed.)*

DANIEL: You've got to wait

DELILAH: Never

DANIEL: I'm going to have to torture you then

DELILAH: Oh shut...*(he starts tickling her.)* Daniel! Daniel...
Mum! Mum!

DANIEL: Shut up you twat she'll think you mean it

DELILAH: I do! I do

He puts his hand over her mouth, they are both laughing, he is tickling her and she is scrabbling away at him on the bed.

SCENE THREE

Friday 8.30pm. The living room, DELILAH fiddles with the TV, DANIEL sprawled on the sofa. NICK enters.

NICK: So this is where you got to

DANIEL sits up.

44

DELILAH: Don't make me clear up please dad

NICK: It's okay your mum is doing it, just don't go in there she'll bite your head off

DELILAH: The Blue Ray bit's broken on the player, when we getting a new one?

NICK: Your mother says you watch the TV too much to start with

DELILAH: But...

NICK: Don't bring it up with me, it's your mum saying it, not me

DELILAH: Can't you talk to her?

NICK: No I'd like to keep my balls

NICK laughs, looks at DANIEL who laughs obligingly.

NICK: What are you watching?

DELILAH: Dark Knight

NICK: Is that that film where that poor young guy died in

DELILAH: Yeah

NICK: I'd like to see that, don't mind, do you?

DELILAH: No

VICKY: *(From offstage.)* Nick! Nick please

NICK: I will actually that would be nice

VICKY: Nick! *(NICK sits.)*

DELILAH: Dad

VICKY comes out.

VICKY: Nick! Didn't you hear me call?

NICK: No

DANIEL: Would you like a hand?

VICKY: No it's alright you watch your film, Nick can you please not just sit there

NICK: I was going to watch this film, leave it Vicky come watch this film too

DELILAH: It's the Dark Knight

VICKY: No it'll be far too violent

DELILAH: I'll tell you when to cover your eyes

VICKY: I don't see how seeing people getting beaten up is entertainment

NICK: Vicky we used to go and see every James Bond film

DANIEL: This is Batman, it's not realistic

DELILAH: Well kind of *(DANIEL makes a sh sign at her.)*

VICKY: Oh well I need to clear up first

NICK: Leave it

VICKY: No because I'll be tired after the film and...

NICK: I'll do it

VICKY: You certainly won't, you'll break all the good glasses

DELILAH: Please mum

VICKY sighs and sits down next to NICK, they are sitting too close so shift away from each other. DELILAH starts the DVD, sits on the floor underneath DANIEL who slowly lies down again on the sofa.

DANIEL: These adverts are a joke

DELILAH: Remember the old ones? 'The pirates are out to get you...

DANIEL and DELILAH: don't let them brand you with their mark'

VICKY: Somebody turn out the lights

No one moves, pause, they all move.

NICK: I'll do it

Lights are turned out; they are lit by the light of the television.

VICKY: What's that in the corner?

DANIEL: Timer

VICKY: What's that?

DELILAH: It's just like the player thing going, ignore it

VICKY: Can't you get rid of it?

DELILAH: No mum watch the film

VICKY: Where's the remote?

DELILAH: I don't know how you do it

VICKY: Give it here

DELILAH: Mum!

VICKY: It will only take a second *(DELILAH reluctantly hands over the remote, VICKY squints.)* Turn a light on Nick

NICK: Vicky for the love of God

DELILAH: Mum sh

VICKY: *(Whispering.)* Nick turn the light on don't be so difficult

DANIEL: I can't remember what happened in the last film

DELILAH: Shall I tell you?

VICKY: If I don't understand it, I'll just go and do the dishwasher

DELILAH: I'll tell you. There's this billionaire called Bruce Wayne and his parents get killed

VICKY: How horrible

DELILAH: Then there's, *(The TV starts bleeping.)* Mum what have you done?

VICKY: I don't know I can't see anything

NICK: Oh give it here Vicky

VICKY: Fine

DELILAH: This black guy who gives him all...

NICK: Now is that Morgan Freeman?

DELILAH: Yeah

NICK: Because I saw him in the trailer once and I wasn't sure if it was for this...

DELILAH: Yeah well it is him and he...

NICK: Morgan Freeman is the one in Driving Miss Daisy isn't he?

DELILAH: I don't know...

NICK: And he's in another film isn't he?

DELILAH: He's in lots of films

DANIEL: Seven, Shawshank Redemption, Bruce Almighty?

NICK: No a film me and Vicky know, what is it called?

VICKY: I've got no idea what you are talking about

NICK: Oh hang on wasn't he in that film with the dinosaurs

DANIEL: That's Samuel L Jackson

VICKY: It doesn't matter

NICK: Big tall black guy?

DANIEL: So's Samuel Jackson

DELILAH: Look he's the guy and...

NICK: I'm sure we'll pick up all this stuff in the film

DELILAH: Okay if you don't understand I'll put it on pause. Dad?

NICK baffled by it passes over the remote, DELILAH starts the film.

VICKY: I'm going to go and get a blanket

NICK: Why?

VICKY: I'm cold

NICK: Delilah will you go and get one for your mum so she doesn't miss it

DELILAH: *(Annoyed.)* Fine *(Leaves.)*

VICKY: Nick the timer is still there

NICK gets up heavily and starts fiddling with the player itself.

VICKY: Well now we can't see anything

NICK: I'm trying to fix it

VICKY: Do you know how?

NICK: I am working it out!

VICKY: Daniel do you know how to do it?

DANIEL: I'm not sure

VICKY: Why don't you give it a go?

NICK: There's no need! No need. I'm doing it, Vicky watch the bloody film and leave me to it

VICKY: I can't leave you to it you are in the way

NICK: *(Bangs the DVD box.)* Oh for God's sake

VICKY: And now you are in the way, about to break the machine and probably the DVD too

NICK: We can still afford a DVD Vicky!

VICKY: For now

NICK: *(Gets up and sits.)* Well you are just going to have to live with the timer then, *(Trying very hard to be patient.)* now can we just, watch the film?

VICKY: Seen this film before then Daniel?

NICK: Obviously not else why would he be watching it?

VICKY: Heard of re-watching films?

DANIEL: Haven't actually seen it before

VICKY: That's a lovely shirt Daniel

NICK: For God's sake Vicky

DELILAH returns, throws a blanket to VICKY.

VICKY: Thanks, oh darling you must be freezing go and get a jumper

DELILAH: I'm fine I got a blanket anyway

DELILAH sits on DANIEL's sofa and shares the blanket with him.

VICKY: Do you want a drink?

NICK: No just watch the film Vicky

VICKY: No I'll enjoy it much more with a drink

DELILAH: Go quick or you won't understand any of it

VICKY: Do you want a drink?

DELILAH: No! Just go

VICKY: Daniel do you want a drink?

DANIEL: No I'm fine

VICKY: You sure?

DANIEL: I'll be okay

NICK: Stop harassing the boy

DELILAH cuddles back with DANIEL.

VICKY: Just me then, is there any of the wine left?

NICK: Sh

VICKY: What?

NICK: I'm watching

VICKY: Is there any wine left?

NICK: What?

VICKY: *(Slowly.)* Is there any wine left?

NICK: No there's the wine box though

VICKY: Thank you, you sure Daniel?

DELILAH: Mum! Stop talking

DANIEL nods, VICKY leaves.

NICK: Sorry about her

DANIEL: It's fine

NICK: Just tell her to shut up if...(*Looks round sees them cuddled up on the sofa, surprised and bemused.*) blimey comfortable enough you two?

DANIEL: (*Pushing DELILAH up.*) Sorry

NICK smiles and turns back to the TV, DELILAH goes to lie back down but DANIEL pushes her up again, a shot on the screen makes them all jump. VICKY returns and sits.

VICKY: (*About the TV.*) What's going on?

DELILAH: You'd know if you'd been here

VICKY: I didn't know we were going to watch this film

NICK: Shut up you two

There is about five seconds during which they watch in silence, DELILAH sinks back down.

VICKY: I don't think this is my sort of film

NICK: You haven't given it a chance

DELILAH: It changes in a minute

VICKY: (*After a short pause.*) Why were they all wearing those masks?

NICK: Vicky shut up and watch the film

VICKY: I am watching the film

NICK: No you're constantly talking about it

VICKY: I don't particularly want to be watching it

DELILAH annoyed and embarrassed puts her head on DANIEL's chest who laughs softly and puts his arms around her. VICKY and NICK are staring at the screen.

NICK: Well no one made you watch it

VICKY: You did

NICK: Yes I strapped you down Vicky

VICKY: I was quite happy clearing away the supper

NICK: No you weren't you came in here to complain I wasn't being your man servant

DELILAH and DANIEL have started half whispering and half mouthing to each other, DELILAH still leaning against him, things like DELILAH – 'they are so embarrassing' and DANIEL – 'it's fine'.

VICKY: It's not being a man servant it's called helping!

NICK: Then why can't you ask me nicely rather than scream like a fucking banshee for me?

VICKY: Why should I do it all and you be my helper why can't it be the other way around?

NICK: Because you won't fucking let me do...

VICKY: Nick no one wants to hear your constant swearing

NICK: Oh yes I'm the one that swears all the fucking time!

VICKY: Not in front of Delilah

NICK: Well aren't you just the perfect mother

VICKY: You are a bloody bastard sometimes

NICK: Ah swearing

VICKY: What?

NICK: Swearing 'bloody bastard'

VICKY: Oh get a life Nick

NICK: I'm sitting here watching this film perfectly happily and out you come and...

VICKY: Ask you to help! What is wrong with that?

NICK: Because I can't help you if you constantly tell me I'm doing it wrong

VICKY: You deliberately do it wrong so you won't have to do it

NICK: Of course I don't

VICKY: Well how many times have I told you not to put the glasses with the rim in the dishwasher?

NICK: Why can't I? Because they might actually get clean if I put them in there?

VICKY: Because they'll break and then the dishwasher will break

NICK: No they won't break I've put them in there plenty of times before

VICKY: Why have you put them in there? I keep asking you not to

DELILAH sits up upset but also trying not to laugh, DANIEL sits up too and hugs her, laughing.

NICK: I don't give a damn about glasses that's why

DELILAH kisses DANIEL.

NICK: Vicky this is stupid just watch the god damn film

DANIEL pushes her away, jumps up

DANIEL: Just going to the bathroom *(DANIEL leaves.)*

NICK: It's so embarrassing arguing in front of him

VICKY: Well it's your fault he's here

DELILAH: I am going to go and get a jumper *(DELILAH leaves.)*

DELILAH and DANIEL stand in the hallway, DANIEL stares speechless, she stands in front of him abashed.

VICKY: To hell with this film

She gets up to leave.

NICK: Vicky, Vicky...Victoria *(She turns furious.)* I'm sorry

VICKY: This really is the bloody end when you call me Victoria

NICK: It's just a name it doesn't mean anything

VICKY: It does mean something! You started calling me Vicky and I thought it was special you said...

NICK: Don't! I know what I said

VICKY: Because your boss was called Victoria you didn't like calling me by the same name and it was so cold compared to Vicky but...

NICK: I know! I know! Why are you telling me again?

VICKY: Actually it was because that bitch didn't like me having the same name as her

NICK: *(Flaring up.)* For God's sake why go on ab...*(Stops himself.)* I'm sorry Vicky

VICKY: I don't know what to say anymore... just leave me alone Nick

NICK: What's the matter with you?

VICKY: I think we all know that

NICK: Don't be so fucking chippy with me. You wouldn't even sit still to watch the film

VICKY almost starts to cry but stops herself.

NICK: Vicky...Vicky sweetheart

VICKY: All I seem to do is fucking cry nowadays and piss everyone off, just leave me alone

NICK: Vicky...

VICKY: Stop whining my fucking name out...I just don't know how to act normally anymore. I can't put it out of my mind. You put your arm round me and... I can't take anyone even being nice to me. I was just thinking about everything, I feel like I've forgotten how to be me

NICK: Don't be stupid

VICKY: Can you stop telling me how stupid and ridiculous I am all the time Nick?

NICK: What do you want?

VICKY: I don't know

NICK: What can I do then?

VICKY: Nick just leave me alone it's fine

NICK: *(Like an insult.)* I do still love you

VICKY: I'll talk to you in the morning

NICK: Vicky can't we just talk about this...

VICKY: What can we say? We've said it all *(Leaving.)*

They stop in the living room, DANIEL and DELILAH outside in the hall.

DANIEL: What the hell was that about?

DELILAH: I don't know

DANIEL: I had no idea, no idea what's so ever

DELILAH: I didn't either

DANIEL: What? How could you not know?

DELILAH: Know what?

DANIEL: I had no idea about the way you felt

DELILAH: Neither did I! I only just thought of it, I suddenly thought of Leonie coming tomorrow then you were really close to me and it was just one of those random thoughts that goes into your head

DANIEL: What are you talking about?

DELILAH: Like if you had tourettes or something

DANIEL: Delilah what the hell?

DELILAH: Like you're in assembly or something and you think what if I yelled out or swore at a teacher or knocked everything off the shelves and I just was sitting there and I thought what if I kissed you and so...

DANIEL: So you did!

DELILAH: I know I know I know I'm sorry

DANIEL: I don't know what to say.

DELILAH: You don't have...I don't know

DANIEL: Oh Del fucking hell

DELILAH: It doesn't matter

DANIEL: Of course it matters. Okay, how do you feel now?

DELILAH: What?

DANIEL: You just said it was impetuousness

DELILAH: What's impet, impete...uousness?

DANIEL: Jesus

DELILAH: What sorry I don't know what a word means

DANIEL: Spur of the moment

DELILAH: Ok

DANIEL: So if it was just a spur of the moment thing then how do you feel now?

DELILAH: I don't know

DANIEL: You don't know how you feel?

DELILAH: No, I only just thought about it. I just did... whatever. I'm so sorry

DANIEL: Stop it Delilah...I'm going to bed

DELILAH: Daniel

DANIEL: What do you want Del? What can I say to make this...

DELILAH: Just don't go

In the living room the pair start again.

NICK: Vicky wait

DELILAH: Daniel please

VICKY: Night

DANIEL: Night Del

VICKY and DANIEL leave. NICK turns feeling useless in the living room and DELILAH re-enters.

NICK: Your mum's clearing the table

DELILAH: Daniel felt ill

NICK: She didn't like the film

DELILAH: He didn't want to be up late

They sit on opposite ends of the sofa staring at the screen, not really watching.

END OF ACT ONE

ACT TWO

SCENE ONE

Saturday, 10am. DANIEL lies on his bed facing the ceiling, LEONIE FOWLER looking in his chest of drawers.

LEONIE: Daniel!

DANIEL: What?

LEONIE: That is absolutely disgusting....Daniel

DANIEL: Hm?

LEONIE: That is absolutely disgusting

DANIEL: What is?

LEONIE: You've got plates of food in your drawers

DANIEL: One

LEONIE: One! Yes one in this drawer but here's another and here's another...

DANIEL: Ok ok

LEONIE: It's absolutely disgusting

DANIEL: Ok ok you're not my mum

LEONIE turns around open mouthed, mock horror.

DANIEL: Aw sorry

LEONIE: You alright? *(Coming over to the bed.)*

DANIEL: What do you mean?

LEONIE: You're a bit...

DANIEL: I'm tired

LEONIE: Aw sweetie

DANIEL: Couldn't sleep

LEONIE: Missing me

DANIEL: Um...

LEONIE: *(Pushes him.)* Fuck you

DANIEL: What?

LEONIE: What?

DANIEL: I was joking

LEONIE: So was I

DANIEL: Oh....sorry

Pause, she lies with him on the bed.

LEONIE: You've changed it

DANIEL: The room?

LEONIE: Yeah I swear the photo showed it all like...

DANIEL: What?

LEONIE: All like different, like the shells and that picture and stuff

DANIEL: I took them down

LEONIE: It was yellow

DANIEL: You got a memory

LEONIE: And that photo of you here from like two...

DANIEL: Vicky said I could paint it

LEONIE: That's nice

DANIEL: Yeah

LEONIE: You must be getting on with them

DANIEL: What do you mean?

LEONIE: I mean they let you paint it and let me come and stay

DANIEL: They just needed to get to know me

LEONIE: Yeah so they must like you

DANIEL: They like me fine

LEONIE: Good

DANIEL: Why do you say it like that?

LEONIE: What?

DANIEL: 'Good'

LEONIE: I didn't say it like anything

DANIEL: Why are you asking me that now?

LEONIE: I dunno. Stop being so touchy

DANIEL: I'm not being touchy

LEONIE: What is it?

DANIEL: Nothing

LEONIE: Snuck...what is it?...Snuck?

DANIEL: I'm fine...I'm fine baby

LEONIE: You don't seem it *(Leans over him.)* Danny?

DANIEL: Don't get in my face *(She laughs unbelievingly, he remembers himself.)* sorry *(He hugs her.)* sorry

LEONIE: *(Kisses him.)* something *(Kiss.)* is *(Kiss.)* the *(Kiss.)* matter...

DANIEL: Nothing!

LEONIE: *(Sits up.)* Danny?

DANIEL: What?

LEONIE: You sad again?

DANIEL: What?

LEONIE: Are you sad again?

DANIEL: Fuck off

LEONIE: Do you want to talk?

DANIEL: I'm not sad

LEONIE: Then what is it?

DANIEL: Nothing

LEONIE: Danny?

DANIEL: What?

LEONIE: Will you sit up when I'm talking to you?

Tentative knock on the door, DANIEL sits up straight away.

LEONIE: Thank you, what...

DANIEL: Del?

LEONIE: Who's...

The knock comes again.

DANIEL: Vicky?

Knock again.

LEONIE: Come in

DELILAH opens the door.

DELILAH: Oh hello

LEONIE gets up off the bed.

LEONIE: Oh hello, who, who are you sweetheart?

DELILAH: Delilah

DANIEL: Their daughter

LEONIE: *(She shoots a look at Daniel.)* Oh hello, I'm, I'm Leonie Danny's friend

DELILAH: Hello

LEONIE: How old are you Delilah?

DANIEL: Twelve

DELILAH: Thirteen tomorrow

LEONIE: Really? You look much older

Pause, DELILAH tries to catch DANIEL's eye who deliberately ignores it.

DANIEL: What do you want?

LEONIE: Danny!

DANIEL: What?

LEONIE: Don't be like that...he's in a grump today, you know what men are like

DELILAH: Mm

LEONIE: So what year are you in at school?

DELILAH: Year 8

LEONIE: So are you doing your GCSEs?

DELILAH: No we choose them next year

DANIEL half groans and half sighs, lies down.

LEONIE: Really? Do you know what you're going to pick?

DELILAH: Have to do some subjects but I'm going to do History, Art and Drama

LEONIE: Oh same as I did

DANIEL rolls over, face in the pillows.

LEONIE: Well um... I guess I'll see you around I'm staying for the week

DELILAH: Daniel?

DANIEL: What?

DELILAH: Are you ok?

DANIEL: Yes why wouldn't I be?

LEONIE: Ignore him, see you later then

DELILAH: Ok

Pause.

LEONIE: You ok?

DELILAH: Yeah

DELILAH goes, LEONIE rounds on DANIEL.

LEONIE: Why didn't you say they had a daughter?

DANIEL: Didn't I?

LEONIE: No you said it was a couple

DANIEL: I did tell you

LEONIE: No

DANIEL: Okay...why does it matter?

LEONIE: It doesn't

DANIEL: So why are you fussing?

LEONIE: I just want to know what's going on with you

DANIEL: Well now you know *(LEONIE hasn't moved even though he is reaching out for her.)* Come here

LEONIE hesitates then comes forward, he pulls her onto the bed and she sits astride him.

LEONIE: Why were you mean to her?

DANIEL: I wasn't was I?

LEONIE: *(Unbelieving.)* Daniel

DANIEL: Alright, I'm sure she won't mind

LEONIE: Why did she come in here?

DANIEL: Oh my God *(He flops back on the bed.)* why do you care! I don't know do I?

LEONIE: Probably besotted *(Kisses his forehead.)*

DANIEL: Get off

LEONIE: She's pretty

DANIEL: What?

LEONIE: Their kid

DANIEL: Mm *(He turns over, face into the pillow.)*

LEONIE: Does she always come in here?

DANIEL: *(Very muffled by the pillow.)* No

LEONIE: I can't hear a fucking word Danny

DANIEL: *(Moves a bit so she can hear.)* Not really

LEONIE: Weird...

DANIEL: She probably wanted to see what you looked like

LEONIE: Mm... *(Prodding him in the back.)* Danny, Danny I've come all this way to see you and you've just got your face

DANIEL: *(Muffled into the pillow.)* I'm sorry

LEONIE: What was that?

DANIEL: Sorry

LEONIE: Didn't quite catch that

DANIEL: *(Pushing her.)* Stop

LEONIE: No I'm sorry what was...

DANIEL half pushes, half tickles so she topples, he turns and pulls her up.

DANIEL: Sorry

LEONIE: Hmm

DANIEL: Sorry

LEONIE faces him half amused.

DANIEL: *(Kisses her and lies back down on his front.)* Sorry

Pause

LEONIE: What's the matter?

DANIEL: Oh shut up

LEONIE: Why won't you...

DANIEL: You're un-fucking-stoppable

She kisses the back of his head. They relax. He turns over.

DANIEL: I've missed you

LEONIE: Really?

DANIEL: Mm

LEONIE: You lost the power of speech Danny?

DANIEL: What?

LEONIE: What's the matter?

DANIEL lies back down

DANIEL: Oh my God!

LEONIE: Is it that girl?

DANIEL: What?

LEONIE: What's her name again Deborah?

DANIEL: Delilah

LEONIE: Yeah

DANIEL: Why would she be the matter?

LEONIE: I don't know do I? I just don't get why you wouldn't tell me about her

DANIEL: I thought I had! You probably forgot

LEONIE: No you didn't

DANIEL: Deepest apologies then babe

DANIEL pulls her down.

LEONIE: You're being such a freak today

Kissing her he starts half murmuring and half humming 'Superfreak' by Rick James which makes her laugh, he pushes her over.

LEONIE: I really don't get you

EMMA M, NAOMI and reluctant EMMA G push the door open to watch, they manage to quietly until EMMA M starts giggling, both LEONIE and DANIEL sit up.

LEONIE: Fuck, I mean Jesus...hello

DANIEL: Oh for God's sake girls

NAOMI: Sorry Daniel we were looking for Delilah

LEONIE: Why would she be in here?

NAOMI: We came over to drop our sleeping bags for tomorrow

DANIEL: She's not in here girls so...

DELILAH down the hall sees them in DANIEL's room.

DELILAH: Why are you in Daniel's room?

NAOMI: We were looking for you in your *friend's* room

DELILAH: Naomi!

DELILAH comes to the door.

DANIEL: Girls do you mind?

EMMA M: Sorry Daniel

EMMA G: Sorry Daniel

They move away embarrassed, DELILAH pushes NAOMI away.

NAOMI: Ow Delilah

DELILAH: Sorry Daniel

LEONIE: It's alright love

DELILAH: Daniel sorry

LEONIE: Danny

DANIEL: Yeah fine get out

She pauses for a moment then shuts the door, you hear from outside.

DELILAH: I fucking hate you guys

EMMA G: Delilah!

EMMA M: But he's your friend

NAOMI and EMMA M laugh, they move off.

LEONIE: *(Quite amused.)* They fucking love you

DANIEL: What?

LEONIE: Don't act like you don't love it

DANIEL: Love what?

LEONIE: Your fans

DANIEL: They're just kids Leonie what the fuck?

LEONIE: Danny don't start again

DANIEL: Can you just fuck off! Jesus

LEONIE: What have I done now? You're such a freak...Danny such a freak *(Crawls up to DANIEL, starts humming the song he stays put till she reaches him.)*

DANIEL: For fuck's sake

He jumps up and leaves LEONIE confused, kneeling on the bed.

SCENE TWO

Saturday 11.30am. In the kitchen LEONIE sits on the table facing DANIEL, she has a cup of tea, they've made up (for now). NICK comes into the room with towels.

NICK: Ah, you're here! I was being sent by the Almighty to give you these

LEONIE: Thank you Mr Evans

NICK: Nick, Nick call me Nick

DANIEL: Yeah thank you

NICK: Everything alright then for both of you?

VICKY: *(Offstage.)* Nick!

LEONIE: Yes completely

NICK: How long did your train take then?

VICKY: Nick for God's sake

LEONIE: Oh I don't know...

DANIEL: Nick Vicky's...

LEONIE: Two three hours

NICK: That's not bad at all actually because I've got to go up to...

VICKY enters with a second towel.

VICKY: What's the point Nick of you helping if I just have to follow you and redo your tasks?

NICK: *(Directing this joke to LEONIE who smiles politely.)* What indeed?

VICKY: Oh you're in here, I was going to come and give you another towel

DANIEL: Thank you

LEONIE: I'll take them in a minute don't worry

LEONIE takes the towels from them both, an awkward pause.

NICK: Delilah says you're going with them swimming tomorrow...Daniel

DANIEL: Oh well...

NICK: *(To VICKY.)* That'll be good won't it?

VICKY: Yes so it'll be just me and Daniel supervising

NICK: Yes it will. Hope you can stand the music Daniel

DANIEL: What?

NICK: That... *(High School Musical music starts from upstairs again.)* Speak of the devil there they go again, I thought the rabble had gone home

VICKY: Naomi's mum is coming at half past

NICK: It is half past

VICKY: It's not yet

NICK: Yes it is look up there

VICKY: That clock is fast

NICK: Why does nothing bloody work in this house?

VICKY: Why 'indeed'?

DANIEL: You not going Nick?

NICK: To what?

DANIEL: Tomorrow

NICK: I um... no

VICKY: Delilah doesn't want him to be there

NICK: No it's not exactly that Vicky

VICKY: He embarrasses her

NICK: No Vicky that isn't...

VICKY: So it's just me and you Daniel

NICK: You've said that Vicky

VICKY: I'm repeating it Nick

NICK: Why? What are you trying to do?

VICKY: What do you think I'm doing?

NICK: Trying to make me jealous perhaps

DANIEL: Come on now

VICKY: No Nick strangely enough I wasn't

DANIEL: Nick

NICK: Really? I was under the impression that the radio every night was actually you and Daniel furtively at it

VICKY: Oh no that's not the radio Nick

NICK: Well God knows how I'm meant to tell the difference

VICKY: What? What Nick you're not even making any bloody sense anymore

DANIEL: Guys please

LEONIE: *(Whispered.)* Danny

LEONIE's voice reminds them all of her presence

NICK: Oh I'm sorry darling

LEONIE: What?

NICK: Sorry we're just being a couple of idiots

VICKY: Ignore him

NICK: Us

VICKY: Just... *(Can't finish the sentence.)*

LEONIE: It's okay

Pause.

VICKY: We'll um...then just leave you to it

NICK: Yes

VICKY: Sorry darling

LEONIE: Oh no it's...

VICKY and NICK bump into each other trying to leave, exit. Close the door and sigh, catch each other's eye and almost laugh. Meanwhile DANIEL looks at LEONIE apologetically.

LEONIE: Well that was...

DANIEL: Bizarre

VICKY: Fucking hell that was...

NICK: Awkward

DANIEL: You know there's nothing...

LEONIE: Yeah

NICK: You're just joking aren't you when you...

VICKY: Oh Nick

DANIEL: She just does it to wind Nick up

NICK: Vicky just give me one straight answer

VICKY: You caught me; I ravage him every night

NICK: Vicky! God... this is such a dysfunctional family

DANIEL: They're just a fucked up family

VICKY: No Nick there is nothing, wish I could have said that about you and...

NICK: Yes, yes, yes I know

They look at each other and not knowing what to do, leave.

DANIEL: Leonie...baby, please

DANIEL puts his arms around her and he talks into her ear.

DANIEL: They're just a couple of old...

LEONIE: So awkward

DANIEL: You're not staying long

LEONIE: Oh great then you'll be left with them again

DANIEL: They'll stop now they've been caught

You hear NAOMI and EMMA G calling goodbye to DELILAH.

LEONIE: Their poor kid

DANIEL: Mm?

LEONIE: You be nice to her Danny

DANIEL: I am

LEONIE: It's what? Her birthday?

DANIEL: Tomorrow

LEONIE: Have you got her a present?

DANIEL: Yes

LEONIE: What? I don't believe you

DANIEL: I have

LEONIE: You still owe *me* a birthday present

DANIEL: Don't start... *(Lets her go.)*

LEONIE: I was joking Danny!

DANIEL: At me again

LEONIE: Joking!

DANIEL: I'll get you one okay but I haven't got much cash right now

LEONIE: It's fine! It was a joke...Danny....Danny

Pause.

LEONIE: What's her name again?

DANIEL: Who?

LEONIE: Their kid

DANIEL: Delilah

LEONIE: What like the song?

DANIEL: What song?

LEONIE: *(Sings the first phrase of 'Hey There Delilah'.)* ...don't you know it?

DANIEL: No

LEONIE: Everyone knows that song Danny

DANIEL: Never heard it before

LEONIE: Really?

DANIEL: No! What's it matter?

EMMA M is pushed into the room.

EMMA M: We're going Daniel

DANIEL: What?

DELILAH enters the room.

DELILAH: Emma!

EMMA M: What?

DELILAH: Naomi's mum is waiting

EMMA M: Bye Daniel

DELILAH: Emma!

EMMA M: Bye Leonie

LEONIE: Bye

EMMA M: I'll miss you *(Starts laughing and runs from the room.)*

DELILAH: Sorry, sorry

DELILAH turns and follows EMMA M off.

DANIEL: Don't say anything!

LEONIE: Okay, okay *(They smile at each other.)*

DANIEL: It's quite embarrassing actually

LEONIE: *(Teasing, she sits on his lap.)* Is it baby?

DANIEL: Yeah

LEONIE: We should play a board game with her

DANIEL: What?

LEONIE: No listen to me, it'll be sweet

DANIEL: Why are you obsessed with her?

LEONIE: I'm not I think it'll be cute

DANIEL: Why?

LEONIE: Because...Danny stop being so difficult

DANIEL: I'm not being difficult if you want to play a board game with her you play a board game with her

LEONIE: Alright alright, will you go and ask her?

DANIEL: Ask her what?

LEONIE: If she wants to play a game or watch a film or something

DANIEL: What the fuck is this Leonie?

LEONIE: Fine I'll go and ask her myself, why are you getting so stressed she's just a kid *(DANIEL groans at the mention of the word kid.)* you know whatever Danny I feel sorry for her so I'm going to ask

DANIEL: No Leonie please

LEONIE's gone. DANIEL jumps up and goes to the door, leans out.

DANIEL: *(Hisses.)* Leonie

DANIEL starts fiddling with things in the kitchen unsure of what to do, returns to the door.

DANIEL: Leonie

Comes back in, swears quietly to himself, tries to find a place to sit in the room then goes to leave as LEONIE enters followed by DELILAH, who he doesn't immediately see.

DANIEL: It's just leading her o...

LEONIE: *(Gives DANIEL a look of daggers.)* Hang on a sec then darling

LEONIE leaves.

DELILAH: What did you say to her?

DANIEL: Nothing

DELILAH: Then why did you just say...

DANIEL: I'm allowed to say whatever I like to my girlfriend Delilah

DELILAH: Shut up!

DANIEL: Where did she go?

DELILAH: Getting a game

DANIEL: Why did you agree?

DELILAH: What did you want me to say?

DANIEL: Fine you sit here and play whatever you want I'm going out

DELILAH: Daniel

DANIEL: What?

DELILAH: Daniel

DANIEL: What? What do you want?

DELILAH: You

DANIEL: Oh shut the fuck up! Did you get that off the OC?

DELILAH: Danny I love you

DANIEL: You're joking

DELILAH: Danny!

DANIEL: You pre-teen stupid idiot. Think this is so romantic? You're fucking with my life you bitch

DELILAH goes to speak then starts crying.

DANIEL: Delilah...Delilah don't...Del, Del stop it. I'm sorry can you please fucking stop

LEONIE comes in but is looking through the box giving DELILAH time to wipe her tears away quickly.

LEONIE: I think all the parts are here you're much better at looking after things than me I always used to lose them *(Looks up.)* everything okay?

SCENE THREE

Saturday 12.30pm. NICK and VICKY in the living room, both reading the papers. NICK has a cup of coffee.

NICK: Huh

VICKY carries on reading.

NICK: Well I didn't know that....did you? Vicky...Vicky?

VICKY: What?

NICK: I never knew that did you?

VICKY: What?

NICK: Listen 'Michael Parkinson never thought that in his long career...'

VICKY: Don't read it to me

NICK: Why?

VICKY: Let me read it

NICK: I'll read it to you

VICKY: I don't like you reading to me

He hands it over grumpily, she reads after a few seconds.

NICK: Isn't that interesting?

VICKY: I haven't finished

NICK: Surely you've read though the part about...

VICKY: Let me finish

NICK: But...

VICKY: Nick please!

NICK: Vicky I haven't finish...

VICKY: Don't start

Pause.

NICK: Finished?

VICKY: No

NICK: You're a slow reader

VICKY tears the paper in two. DELILAH comes in.

DELILAH: When's lunch?

VICKY: What time's it?

DELILAH: Twelve thirty

NICK: What!

NICK jumps up spilling his coffee onto VICKY.

VICKY: Nick! You just burnt me

NICK: What?

VICKY: You spilt it

NICK: Oh I'm really sorry get a cloth Delilah

DELILAH leaves.

VICKY: Nick!

NICK: What?

VICKY: You get the bloody cloth Nick

NICK: What?

VICKY: Stop bleating what

NICK: I can't laze around all day

VICKY: I came to read the papers and you followed me. And you've just burnt me

NICK: Oh I'm sorry you've been crippled

VICKY: No *(She gets up.)* Miracle I can walk

NICK: Hallelujah

VICKY: Yes praise the fucking lord

DELILAH comes in and gives VICKY the cloth and leaves, she leaves and knocks on DANIEL's door.

NICK: I was going to go to the market

VICKY: The market? Go to the goddamn Job Centre

She opens the door, DANIEL is sitting on the edge of his bed in his boxers and t-shirt smoking a cigarette.

NICK: It's the weekend Vicky

VICKY: You slept through the alarm

NICK: What alarm!

VICKY goes to retort but stops short, and leaves instead, NICK turns after her.

NICK: Vicky!

VICKY has gone, NICK shuffles awkwardly in the living room. DELILAH shuts the door. DELILAH and DANIEL, silence.

DELILAH: Where is she?

DANIEL: Gone to the shops

DELILAH: To get what?

DANIEL: You don't want to know

Pause.

DELILAH: You shouldn't be smoking in here

DANIEL: She's getting air freshener as well

DELILAH: Tell her to get the one that's an odour eliminator

DANIEL: What

DELILAH: 'Some air fresheners cover up the bad smells but Oust gets rid of them on impact' or maybe that's Febreeze

DANIEL: You done?

DELILAH: I'm trying to help

DANIEL: Well don't bother yourself

DELILAH: My dad will smell it he's like a blood hound

DANIEL: Was that them arguing again?

DELILAH: Yes

DANIEL: What about?

DELILAH: Cloths

DANIEL half laughs, DELILAH is encouraged.

DELILAH: Sorry

DANIEL: It's alright

DELILAH: I really am

DANIEL: It's fine...I'm sorry about earlier, I...over reacted

DELILAH: It's okay

DANIEL: I let it wind me up

DELILAH: Sorry about my friends too

DANIEL: *(Laughs.)* Yeah, well, whatever

Pause.

DELILAH: Can I have a cigarette?

DANIEL: Can you fuck!

DELILAH: I've had one before

DANIEL: Liar

DELILAH: Emma M had one before

DANIEL: Ah I see then take the pack

DELILAH: I will

DANIEL: You do that

DELILAH: I have

DANIEL: I wish you many returns of your cancer

DELILAH: Take that back

DANIEL: What?

DELILAH: The cancer thing I'll get really worried

DANIEL: Yes me saying it will make it happen

DELILAH: No please take it back it'll stay in my mind and what if I do die from cancer and it's your fault because you said it like a gypsy curse or...

DANIEL: Oh I see

DELILAH: Take it back

DANIEL: I can't guarantee you not getting cancer

DELILAH: Please *(Kneels up on bed.)*

DANIEL: No

DELILAH: Please

DANIEL: If you insist on smoking

DELILAH: I won't

DANIEL: You won't smoke?

DELILAH: No never

DANIEL: Liar

DELILAH: No

DANIEL: You swear never to touch a cigarette, never have a little drag just to see what it's like, never...

DELILAH: No

DANIEL: *(Kneels back on bed.)* No?

DELILAH: Never

DANIEL: Ever?

They are kneeling face to face

DELILAH: Ever

DANIEL impulsively kisses her, delighted she responds. DANIEL pulls away still holding on to her.

DANIEL: *(More to himself than her.)* What the fuck?

She kisses him again, he responds, pulls away again.

DANIEL: What is wrong with me?

DELILAH: Nothing

DANIEL: Why the hell did I just do that?

DELILAH: It doesn't matter

Again she kisses him and pulls him back on to the bed, he allows it to happen, between kisses some of which he initiates and some she does.

DANIEL: What the fuck am I doing? .... what am I doing?...
Stop....Stop...this is the worst thing...ever done....fuck, fuck
(Finally pulling himself together he sits up.) fuck, fuck, fuck

DELILAH: Don't stop

DANIEL: Shit

DANIEL is now sitting on top of her on the bed, he runs his fingers through his hair.

DELILAH: What?

DANIEL: What the fuck am I doing?

DELILAH: *(Trying to pull him back.)* Kissing me

DANIEL: *(Looks at her blankly.)* This is the worst thing I've ever done

DELILAH: It's not

DANIEL: The worst thing I ever could do

DELILAH: No

DANIEL: What about Leonie?

DELILAH: Fucking patronising ugly bitch

DANIEL: Fuck

DELILAH: What?

DANIEL: Like that matters

DELILAH: Yeah it doesn't matter now *(Tries to kiss him.)*

DANIEL: No you stupid little kid it doesn't matter because she
is the last of my...I mean fuck!

DELILAH: Daniel...Danny

Kisses him, he lets her without thinking, not even looking at her then...

DANIEL: What if this was one of your friends?

DELILAH: You like one of my friends?

DANIEL: No!

DELILAH: What do you mean?

DANIEL: What would you think if you were one of your friends?

DELILAH: You like one of them? You like Naomi don't you?

DANIEL: No no Del of course I don't they're just kids

DELILAH: Yeah

DELILAH: Danny

DANIEL: You're just a...

DELILAH: No I'm not! Don't! My friends don't know you, they're not like me *(Kisses him.)* I'm different *(Kisses him again.)* I'm special *(Kisses him then...)*

DANIEL: You don't even know me

DELILAH: Yes I do!

DANIEL: You don't know anything about me, you're just a fucking kid

DELILAH: No I'm not, I know just as much about you as she does

DANIEL: You're a kid, you're a kid

DELILAH: *(Sits up from under him.)* Stop saying that, I love you

DANIEL: A kid!

DELILAH: Stop alright

DANIEL: A little kid, you haven't even done your GCSEs yet!

DELILAH: *(Growing more annoyed.)* So? I know what I want! You don't grow a brain after you turn 16

DANIEL: You're a kid

DELILAH: *(Kisses his neck.)* I'm not

DANIEL: How do you even know to do that?

DELILAH: What?

DANIEL: *(Holds her off.)* What am I doing? *(Kisses her again.)* Worst thing I've ever done

DELILAH: No it's not

DANIEL: How do you know? You don't know me

DELILAH: What is there to know? You're not the fucking Count of Monte Cristo! You aren't all that interesting and mysterious that you can say, 'you don't know me at all'. What's so amazing? Whatever you think is so interesting I'm sure another person could double

DANIEL starts laughing.

DELILAH: See?

Kisses him again; he is almost in tears, kissing her savagely back and pushes her down. He suddenly forces himself away looking into her face still holding her to the bed, long pause.

DANIEL: *(Suddenly he starts to speak half to punish himself and half to punish her.)* I'm a pathetic loser. I'm a bad person. Really...you wouldn't believe how bad I am. I...I'm a...I used to lose my temper at home and hit my dad not even for real reasons just self indulgence. Once left the dog food can open and my dog got hold of it cut his face up with the edge of the can and got stuck in it, blood all over the kitchen my parents were out so I just left him over night. Spat at my old girlfriend in the face to make her leave me because I just didn't want to see her anymore, I'd just be mad at her whenever I saw her. No reason, she hadn't done anything. I lie all the time. Haven't done any of my essays for uni. I've cut myself before I don't even know why I just... I just did and Leonie thinks it was because of her but it wasn't and so she feels like she has to stay with me even though, even though she isn't the problem. She's the best person I've ever met and she loves me but I can't love her, I've tried I really am trying but she, she just, she's so fucking irritating..... I say I don't believe in God but I think I actually do, I just say it to be different... Can't afford your parent's rent. I...I... *(Running out of confessional steam.)* And for some reason I can't stop myself, just like your tourettes thing I keep thinking I don't care anymore 'so what' so I kiss you even though I feel sick and it's so wro... and...and...You don't love me so much now do you?

DELILAH: I do

DANIEL: You just think I'm cool now don't you, 'cause you think I'm screwed up

DELILAH: No

DANIEL: Yes you do...you do

DELILAH: No

DANIEL: But I don't care

He kisses her, even he doesn't know why; desire, punishment, comfort, maybe even love.

SCENE FOUR

Saturday 1pm. VICKY sits on the sofa watching the daytime TV, she watches quietly for a time then slowly starts to cry, NICK comes in with a drink for himself and a coffee for her.

NICK: Here's your bloody... *(Sees her.)* hey, hey, hey come on love

VICKY: Leave me alone Nick

NICK: Vicky I don't know what to do any...

The phone rings, both think about leaving it then NICK rises.

NICK: It might be someone calling back

VICKY: Obviously

NICK: I mean after an interview

VICKY: It's a Saturday Nick

NICK: Oh

VICKY: 'It's the weekend'

The phone still rings.

VICKY: Oh for God's sake

VICKY gets up and answers the phone.

VICKY: Hello? Oh okay, let me just get her *(Calling.)* Delilah! Yes she's just coming

NICK: Is it for Delilah?

VICKY: Obviously or why else would I be calling her? Delilah! It's...

NICK: It's the telephone for you

VICKY: Nick!

DELILAH enters.

DELILAH: Alright! *(Takes the phone.)* Thanks...you don't have to stay

VICKY: Okay!

VICKY leaves, NICK thinks then follows her.

DELILAH: Yeah hi... I dunno that's ages away. No please don't I hate going on speake...Hi. I don't care what you wear...clothes... *(Smiling.)* What? Maybe. Um you three and Jess and Immy and Ayesha and Emily and um...What do you three want to bring anyone? No well no guys apart from... *(Savouring every moment.)* Well um...my boyfriend... yeah...er...yeah I do. Today...don't be like that. Yeah you are you're like 'oh' like you know anything. Well I do from today...

NAOMI, EMMA M and G appear (the other end of the line) EMMA G is painting EMMA M's nails. They have the phone out on speaker.

NAOMI: Have you pulled him?

DELILAH: Yes

EMMA M and G scream in delight.

NAOMI: Properly?

DELILAH: Yeah lots we were just kissing like two hours ago

NAOMI grabs up the phone taking it off speaker.

EMMA M: Naomi!

NAOMI: Who?

EMMA G: Hold still

EMMA M: You're fucking useless at this

NAOMI: Will you be careful with that, don't spill it

EMMA M: Can you be careful!

EMMA G: You wash your hands after and get it off the sides it doesn't matter

NAOMI: Delilah who's your 'boyfriend'?

EMMA G: Who is it?

DELILAH holds the phone away so happy to be able to say.

DELILAH: Daniel

NAOMI: *(Shocked.)* What?

EMMA M: Who is it?

DELILAH: Daniel

EMMA G: Naomi!

NAOMI: You're joking...Delilah

EMMA M: Who is it?

DELILAH: No he's my boyfriend

NAOMI: He can't be

EMMA M: Who?

NAOMI: You're lying

EMMA G: Naomi! Oh my God can you just tell us

DELILAH: I'm not lying why would I be lying?

EMMA M: Who is it?

NAOMI: Daniel

EMMA G: What?

NAOMI: That's disgusting

DELILAH: No it's not

NAOMI: If your parents knew

DELILAH: I'm not going to tell them!

NAOMI: He could get in so much trouble

DELILAH: How would they find out?

NAOMI: But Del...

DELILAH: Just 'cause you like him, just because you're jealous

EMMA M: Let me talk to her

NAOMI: Delilah Daniel is like...

DELILAH: Shut up what do you know? Just jealous that I have
a boyfriend and you don't

EMMA M: Give me the phone Naomi *(Knocks over the nail
polish.)*

EMMA G: Emma!

NAOMI: Emma fucking hell my mum will kill me

DELILAH: You said he was hot

NAOMI: Emma get a cloth or something

DELILAH: My parents are like 7 years apart

NAOMI: Oh my God and it's blue polish!

DELILAH: Bye

NAOMI: Yeah I'll call you later...Emma don't just sit there can
you get something

*The girls disappear, DELILAH is left in the room by the phone. She
sits for a while, NICK enters.*

NICK: Have you seen my tea?

DELILAH: What?

NICK: Must have put it down somewhere, it'll be stone cold by the time I find...ah here it is! Look alive Del was right under your nose, eurgh quite right freezing cold, Del?

DELILAH: Mm

NICK: Cheer up sweetheart... what did the rabble want with you on the phone?

DELILAH: Just stuff about tomorrow

NICK: Oh right... have a tiff with them?

DELILAH: *(Absent minded.)* Not really they're just jealous because I have a boyfriend. *(DELILAH gets up.)* I'm going upstairs

NICK: You have a boyfriend?

DELILAH: Mm *(Quickly.)* no one you know it's...

NICK: *(Bit embarrassed.)* No, no your business

DELILAH: I'm going upstairs

NICK: Chin up

DELILAH: Mm

DELILAH leaves, NICK takes a sip of his tea, thinks.

NICK: Vicky...Vicky

VICKY: *(Offstage.)* What?

NICK: Vicky!

VICKY enters.

VICKY: What?

NICK: *(Smiling but surprised.)* You know Delilah's got a boyfriend

VICKY: What?

NICK: Just told me. Bit young isn't she?

VICKY: Nick she's twelve!

NICK: I know but still a bit young

VICKY: No Nick I mean she is twelve years old what the hell do you mean she has a boyfriend

NICK: Alright calm down love

VICKY: Nick she is twelve! twelve

NICK: Almost thirteen

VICKY: Don't be ridiculous that isn't the point

NICK: Well I thought it was a bit odd

VICKY: A boyfriend an actual boyfriend

NICK: That's what she said, was having an argument saying that lot were just jealous

VICKY: How can she? She's a child

NICK: Blimey I hope she hasn't...

VICKY: Hasn't what?

NICK: Well you know hasn't... *(Almost whispers.)* had sex

VICKY: Nick that's disgusting she is a child

NICK: Well you hear about these things

VICKY: But not to...girls like her

NICK: Well it's bloody ridiculous this

VICKY: What does she think she is playing at! The first boy I ever kissed I was fourteen not twelve, not even a teenager yet

NICK: I wonder who this boy is

VICKY: I'll ring up his parents

NICK: She can't be off with boys at her age it isn't right

VICKY: She's much, much too young

NICK: Delilah!

VICKY: No what are we going to say?

NICK: Delilah come down here right now!

VICKY: What did you say to her when she told you?

NICK: I didn't really say anything to be honest

VICKY: That is so typical Nick

Hearing the shouting, DANIEL comes out of his bedroom listening.

NICK: Delilah get down here this minute! No it isn't typical Vicky there is nothing typical about this

VICKY: You need me to tell you that it is a repulsive thing for a twelve year old child to be off with boys and not just that but showing off about them unashamedly

NICK: Yes I know and I'm going to tell her so

DELILAH enters.

DELILAH: What?

VICKY: Your father just told me that you were talking to that Naomi girl about some boyfriend you think you have

DELILAH: Dad!

VICKY: He has every right to tell me Delilah

NICK You know the first boy your mother kissed she was fourteen not twelve

DELILAH: What? It's nothing to do with…

NICK: You know I think it's a pretty repulsive thing for a twelve year old child to be off with boys and, *(VICKY is looking at him, he loses confidence for a second but continues.)* not, not just that but showing off about them unashamedly

DELILAH: Dad…

NICK: Some great bloody romance at twelve years old

DELILAH turns away.

NICK: Don't just walk off Delilah

VICKY: Delilah

NICK: Delilah come back here right now

DELILAH comes out and slams the door crying and runs upstairs to her room not even seeing DANIEL who doesn't move from outside his room. He leans against the door and slides down and half sings, half hums 'Hey There Delilah' to himself.

VICKY: Nicely handled Nick

NICK: Oh for God's sake *(Smashes something.)*

NICK and VICKY square up again as DANIEL continues to sing.

END OF ACT TWO

ACT THREE

SCENE ONE

Sunday 9.30am. LEONIE is asleep in bed, DANIEL is leaning out their door whispering frustratedly to DELILAH who is just outside

DANIEL: Go! Can you just go?

DELILAH: No I want to talk to you

DANIEL: I can't talk to you

DELILAH: Why? Because of that bitch in there sleeping

DANIEL: Fuck her! I can't talk to you, I can't look at you, just go away

DELILAH: Danny please

DANIEL comes out of his room leaving LEONIE there and forces her into her own room. He follows and holds the door closed behind him.

DANIEL: Stop calling me Danny

DELILAH: Will you say happy birthday

DANIEL: What?

DELILAH: Say happy birthday to me

DANIEL: This is just a joke to you

DELILAH: No it's not!

DANIEL: Can you just fuck off Delilah?

DELILAH: Why what is so wrong with me?

DANIEL: You're a kid, I can't...

DELILAH: I'm not! I'm thirteen, today!

DANIEL: What I did yesterday was the most disgusting, the most...

DELILAH: Amazing thing

DANIEL: Stop! Just stop

DELILAH: Are you only upset because I'm younger than you?

DANIEL: Only!

DELILAH: Daniel

DELILAH tries to kiss him, he shoves her away so violently she trips over and falls.

DELILAH: Daniel

DANIEL: I've had enough of this Delilah do you hear me? I really have, you're pushing me too far. You're a kid

DELILAH: I'm not I'm not

DANIEL: You are, you fucking are. Why are you doing this to me?

DELILAH: I'm not doing anything and I'm not a kid Daniel

DELILAH is still on the floor and DANIEL is leaning over her.

DANIEL: You are twelve, I can barely say it twelve years old. Do you have no idea...

DELILAH: Thirteen!

DANIEL: Delilah for fuck's sake

DELILAH: I'm thirteen! And it's my birthday

DANIEL: Can you not hear how young that is...twelve, thirteen whatever!

DELILAH: Stop it I love you

DANIEL: You're a child

DELILAH: Stop, stop, stop it

DANIEL: A little child

DELILAH slaps DANIEL, both of them are almost crying.

DELILAH: I'm not, I'm not a child

DANIEL: You are Del, how can I have done this to you?

DELILAH: It's my birthday stop being so horrible to me on my birthday!

DANIEL: Oh Del

DELILAH starts hitting him.

DELILAH: I'm not a child, I love you, I love you...

DANIEL: I'm sorry, I'm sorry I should never have...

DELILAH: I'm not a child

DANIEL: I know, it's okay, Del, Del...

DANIEL hugs DELILAH who was still hitting him, he kisses her trying to comfort then realises what he's done. He pulls away and says quietly.

DANIEL: Fuck... *(Anger surges up and he shouts.)* Fuck!

DANIEL punches out at the wall, DELILAH tries to hug him but he hits out at her, they struggle for a second before DANIEL breaks away and heads towards his own room. A door opens further down the corridor and DANIEL bolts into his own room, DELILAH follows but is stopped as she sees NICK come out of his bedroom. DELILAH wipes her face, DANIEL listens at the door, LEONIE stirs in bed.

NICK: Morning

DELILAH: Mm

NICK: Happy birthday sweetheart

DELILAH: Thank you

NICK: Come give your dad a hug

They hug.

NICK: Still not happy with you Delilah though

DELILAH: I know

NICK: And watch out for your mother she's on the warpath

DELILAH: Okay

NICK: She'll cheer up for later though, probably you'll just be a present down

DELILAH: Mm

As NICK exits he says:

NICK: And turn down your TV I could hear a whole lot of yelling

DELILAH: Fine

NICK leaves. DELILAH opens DANIEL's door but LEONIE sits up, seeing this DANIEL holds the door closed against her.

LEONIE: Morning baby

DANIEL: Yeah

LEONIE: Danny...Danny!

DANIEL: I'll get you a cup of tea

LEONIE: Fuck tea come here Danny

DANIEL is torn between letting go of the door which would let DELILAH in and going to her.

DANIEL: Just let me get it

LEONIE: Danny *(She closes her eyes and makes a 'I want a hug' gesture.)*

DANIEL lets go of the door, runs over and kisses her quickly then runs back out just as DELILAH was about to open the door.

LEONIE: Danny?

DANIEL pushes DELILAH into her room again but stays himself out in the corridor, unwilling to engage in the conversation, LEONIE starts to get dressed in DANIEL's room.

DANIEL: Fuck off Del

DELILAH: Can you just stop it?

DANIEL: I'm going to leave

DELILAH: What?

DANIEL: I'm going to leave, move out, go home

DELILAH: No, why?

DANIEL: Why do you fucking think?

DELILAH: You can't I won't let you

DANIEL: Do you not understand how serious this is? You're twelve years old I could go to prison

DELILAH: We just kissed

DANIEL: I know but...

DELILAH: They don't send people to prison for kissing do they?

DANIEL: That's not the fucking point *(Mindlessly one hand has moved to his arm.)*

DELILAH: You didn't

DANIEL: What?

DELILAH: You didn't hurt yourself because of this

DANIEL doesn't understand, he sees her looking at his arm, vicious.

DANIEL: Over you? Who the fuck do you think you are? Another girl that thinks I give a fuck about them

DELILAH: Stop it

DANIEL: And I don't do that

DELILAH: You said you did

DANIEL: Once and what does it matter to you?

DELILAH: Over Leonie

DANIEL: No it wasn't

DELILAH: Over that bitch

DANIEL: You think I would do something like that for you, you are a child

DELILAH: Do you love her?

DANIEL: Yes

DELILAH: You said you didn't

DANIEL: I lied

DELILAH: You're lying now!

LEONIE, half dressed, follows DANIEL out of the room; sees him half in her room.

LEONIE: Danny?

DANIEL backs out of her room, tries to close the door on DELILAH but she comes out.

LEONIE: Oh hello Delilah

DELILAH: Hi

LEONIE: Danny come back

DANIEL: No you go fucking back

LEONIE: Danny!

DANIEL: Go back in the fucking room

LEONIE: Danny stop it

DANIEL: Go back to bed

LEONIE: What?

DANIEL: I'm making you a fucking drink can you just go to bed

LEONIE: What's the matter with you?

DANIEL: Please

LEONIE: Fine fine okay. You alright sweetheart?

DELILAH: Yeah

LEONIE goes back into the room with a push from DANIEL. DANIEL moves down the corridor and goes down into the kitchen, DELILAH follows.

DANIEL: I'm going to tell your parents I've got some family problem and go away

DELILAH: For how long?

DANIEL: I wouldn't come back you idiot *(He puts the kettle on.)*

DELILAH: Don't be stupid Danny *(Tries to touch him but he shoves her away.)*

DANIEL: Stop it! Stop it Delilah stop fucking me over

DELILAH: Danny you can't, I won't let you

DELILAH: Daniel

DANIEL: What can you do?

DELILAH: I'll tell my parents

There's a pause. LEONIE opens the door, looks for DANIEL on the corridor.

LEONIE: Daniel?

LEONIE shuts the door.

DANIEL: Del...

DELILAH: I will I swear to God

DANIEL: Don't, please Del I'm begging you, you can't...

DELILAH: Don't leave then

DANIEL: I can't stay here

DELILAH: Please Daniel I love you, it's my birthday

DANIEL: Christ Delilah you don't get what you're doing

DELILAH: I do! I'm not stupid and I'm not a kid

DANIEL: You don't otherwise you wouldn't...

DELILAH: I wouldn't be doing this! I love you, you have to stay or I'll tell my parents. You don't have to be nineteen *(Indicating Leonie.)* to understand that. Where's the tea then?

DANIEL: Del...

DELILAH: You love me you won't go

DANIEL: You love me you won't tell

DELILAH: I'm not letting you go!

DANIEL goes upstairs, he goes to open the door but DELILAH has followed him, he holds the door shut, LEONIE goes to the door.

DANIEL: Del please...

LEONIE tries to open the door but DANIEL gets there just in time and holds it shut.

DELILAH: It's my birthday

DANIEL: Oh my God

DELILAH: Please Daniel I love you

DANIEL: Del...

DELILAH: You can't go

LEONIE wrenches the door open and DELILAH turns away, DANIEL reluctantly follows LEONIE inside their room.

LEONIE: Danny what the hell is wrong with you?

DANIEL: *(Losing his temper.)* Nothing! How many times?

SCENE TWO

Sunday 10.30am. In the living room, DELILAH is sitting with EMMA G, they're eating something, LEONIE is sitting in DANIEL's room trying to read a folder of work but keeps glancing at DANIEL who is listening to music from his laptop and typing.

EMMA G: How long till the others come?

DELILAH: Like in an hour and a half

EMMA G: Okay

DELILAH: Is your granddad going to be okay?

EMMA G: Yeah mum said it was just his hand he hurt nothing else

DELILAH: Did he land on his hand?

EMMA G: Mum said he like went over on it and cracked it or something *(Demonstrates.)*

DELILAH: Ow

EMMA G: No he's always going to the hospital mum just wanted to get him checked and they wait ages to see a doctor

DELILAH: Where's your dad?

EMMA G: At Tescos and I didn't want to be late, is your mum mad?

DELILAH: No she's just in a weird mood

EMMA G: Really?

DELILAH: She was just annoyed to make food, not at you coming early

EMMA G: You sure?

DELILAH: Yeah

EMMA G: Delilah...

DELILAH: What?

EMMA G: I don't know how to say it

DELILAH: *(Joking.)* What's up blud?

EMMA G: Are you really going out with Daniel?

DELILAH: Mm

EMMA G: You weren't lying?

DELILAH: No

EMMA G: Do your parents know?

DELILAH: That I've got a boyfriend yeah, they went mental

EMMA G: But they don't know it's Daniel

DELILAH: No and you can't tell anyone Emma

EMMA G: Okay

DELILAH: You really can't you've got to promise

EMMA G: Shouldn't you tell your parents though?

DELILAH: Are you stupid?

EMMA G: No but...Del...he's really old

DELILAH: Are you actually stupid Emma? No I can't tell them I would never tell them *(Realising this is true.)* I would never tell them

LEONIE: Danny...Danny can we...

DANIEL: *(Frustrated, gestures that he is concentrating on the screen.)* Hang on

EMMA G: This is really wrong Del

DELILAH: He's hot, you said he was hot

EMMA G: Del...

DELILAH: And he's clever and really interesting and I love him

EMMA G: That's sick

DELILAH: Shut up Emma you're as bad as Naomi

EMMA G: But Delilah this is really wrong

DELILAH: Shut up what would you know Emma, go back to making fucking ringtones for High School Musical

EMMA G: I hate High School Musical you're the one that was doing...

DELILAH: Whatever shut up!

LEONIE: Danny? *(DANIEL ignores her.)*

EMMA G: You're just a kid

DELILAH: Can everyone please stop saying that! Go away

EMMA G: What?

DELILAH: Can you just go away I wish I'd never invited you

EMMA G: You can't un-invite me

DELILAH: Go away

EMMA G: Delilah you're so mean

LEONIE abandons her folder and climbs over to DANIEL who is concentrating on the screen.

DELILAH: Go away you're spoiling my birthday

EMMA G: Delilah!

DELILAH: Go away I'm not a kid and you don't know what you're talking about

EMMA G jumps up and goes out, walking into VICKY who has cupcakes for them. LEONIE puts her arms around DANIEL who jumps, not realising she was so close.

DANIEL: Jesus Christ, get off me

EMMA G: I'm just going to the bathroom

LEONIE: What?

VICKY: Okay love *(EMMA G leaves.)*

LEONIE: You're not talking

DANIEL: I'm working! Give me a minute

LEONIE gets up off the bed, he goes back to typing.

VICKY: Everything okay?

DELILAH: Yeah

VICKY: She looked very unhappy, her granddad's okay isn't he?

DELILAH: Yeah

VICKY: You had a spat with her?

DELILAH: No

VICKY: Oh Del don't be grumpy, I forgot how you girls argue when you're your age

DELILAH: What?

VICKY: Well think I never argue with my friends do I? It's just your age darling don't be upset. You're not crying are you Delilah? Not on your birthday

DELILAH: No... *(Suddenly.)* I'm not too young for a boyfriend am I?

VICKY: Not this again

DELILAH: I'm not mum

VICKY: You are darling...look there's no need to cry about it

LEONIE: You're not even fucking working!

DANIEL: For fuck's sake *(Slams his laptop shut and gets off the bed, he starts looking for his shoes.)*

DELILAH: I wish I was older

VICKY: You won't when you are

DELILAH: I'm not too young mum

VICKY: You just want to grow up too fast

DELILAH: Mum listen...

VICKY: I always was in such a rush to grow up and I never thought about what I'd do when I got there

DELILAH: Mum I'm not too young

LEONIE: What are you doing?

DANIEL: Going outside

LEONIE: What for?

DANIEL: *(Leaving the room.)* Do I have to tell you every fucking thing I'm doing

LEONIE comes out onto the corridor.

DANIEL: Can you not follow me!

He goes downstairs, LEONIE has no shoes on so goes back into DANIEL's room to find some.

VICKY: Oh dear listen to them go

DELILAH: Mum Daniel...

VICKY: I thought they'd stopped

DELILAH: They started again. Mum...

VICKY: There's another couple that don't belong together, oh come here darling

VICKY sits with DELILAH hugging her but not listening to her, trapped in her own thoughts.

DELILAH: Mummy...

VICKY: Darling all this worry about boyfriends they're just silly little boys and it's a waste of your time

DELILAH: He's not a silly little boy

VICKY: No I know sweetheart but honestly there is plenty of time for you to go off and get your heartbroken

DELILAH: Too late

VICKY: Now that's a bit overdramatic isn't it?

DELILAH: Please listen

VICKY: No you think I don't know what I'm talking about Delilah but I do I really do. And you can see it with that Leonie and Daniel they're going just the same way as me and your father

LEONIE heads downstairs.

DELILAH: Mum please don't start

VICKY: But Delilah me and your father are a perfect example. We just didn't know enough when we got married we'd only ever really been serious about each other

DELILAH: Mum we're talking about me

VICKY: Alright, alright I've just got no one to talk to Del and you're my little girl and I don't want... *(NICK comes in unseen by VICKY but seen by DELILAH.)*

DELILAH: Don't be upset

VICKY: It's all such a mess Del all such a big fucking mess

DELILAH: No mummy don't...

VICKY: I mean I love your father so much and it's all wrong because of that bloody woman

DELILAH: Mummy he didn't mean it

VICKY: But he did darling

DELILAH: He didn't *(NICK goes to talk but DELILAH signals for him to not.)*

VICKY: He just thinks I'm this stupid old woman who nags away and doesn't love him but I really, really do Del

DELILAH: He loves you too

VICKY: I wish he did but how could he after everything

DELILAH: He does

VICKY: It's always us playing games and fighting and squabbling and we can never just say what we mean because it's always in an argument

Outside you can hear:

DANIEL: Can't I have one minute to myself

LEONIE: Danny why are you doing this?

DELILAH: Well why don't you talk to him?

NICK tries to talk again but DELILAH stops him.

VICKY: I can't, he doesn't want to, he doesn't want to talk to me because...he just...doesn't love me anymore *(VICKY starts to cry properly.)*

DELILAH: Mummy please

VICKY: I love him and all he does is hate me for everything. I just drove him away and...and...I love him Del and everyone hates me

DELILAH: That's so stupid

VICKY: They do, they really do because I go at everyone

DELILAH: I love you

VICKY: Nick hates me

DELILAH: Mummy he does love you he really does

VICKY: Does he?

LEONIE re-enters the house with a slam of the door and goes back to DANIEL's room.

DELILAH: Yes

VICKY: Then why doesn't he say it? Why does he just use it against me in every argument 'yes but I love you' and I've said 'I'm sorry'

DELILAH: He's scared that you don't love him

VICKY: No he's not, he knows I do

NICK: I don't

VICKY turns and sees NICK.

VICKY: Oh go away Nick

NICK: But Vicky...

VICKY: No all these kids are coming in a minute and...

DELILAH: Can you just listen to him?

VICKY: No see already you two are together; get stupid Vicky to listen to kind old Nick who just made a mistake

NICK: No Vicky...

VICKY: Everyone thinks that you are so good, good but naughty, Nick got caught out cheating on his wife but look at her, look what a stupid mess she is, can you blame him?

NICK: Vicky no one thinks that, don't say anything, no one thinks that. Everyone thinks stupid balding Nick what a pathetic loser, couldn't even get a young pretty girl had to go for an ugly slut and then got fired what an idiot because look at his wife...

VICKY: Shut up shut up no they don't say that you idiot, you think lying to me...

NICK: Vicky since when do you care what everyone else thinks?

VICKY: It's just so embarrassing

NICK: Fine let it be

VICKY: Nick...

NICK: No let it be, we'll be embarrassed together, we'll be the talk of the playground and...

VICKY: Shut up Nick you are so...

NICK: No Vicky, look...I, I really do love you

VICKY: You're just saying that because...

NICK: Why?

DELILAH: Why would he just be saying that?

NICK: Delilah, can you just leave us to it for a minute?

DELILAH: I'm only trying to help

VICKY: I know sweetheart

NICK: Run up to your room for a minute

DELILAH leaves.

NICK: I've forgotten what I was saying now

VICKY: That you love me

NICK: Oh yes *(Despite themselves they laugh.)* Look you stupid woman I love you, I really, really, really do love you. Please, please don't leave me don't let me lose you

VICKY: This is so clichéd Nick

NICK: Fine then let it be clichéd, I am a cliché. I love you, I don't know what more I can say

VICKY: Nick...

NICK: Do you love me?

VICKY: Of course I love you Nick...of course I do, you think I would put up with all this shit if I didn't love you?

NICK: So I love you and you love me, what's the problem?

VICKY: Should have thought of that Nick before...

NICK: No don't please, Vicky just leave it, leave it aside for just one moment, just look at everything, us, without that

VICKY: You are so simplistic Nick, you're such a stupid old simplistic man

NICK: That's what you love about me

VICKY: No it's not

NICK: It is, I make everything simple

VICKY: Until I get away and realise all the crap you've been talking to me

NICK: Fine Vicky, fine. But just for now, let me fill your head with crap and you can be happy for half an hour

VICKY: Less

NICK: Fine less, but it's been a long time since you've let me...

VICKY: Fill my head with crap

NICK: Yes, so things are improving at last

NICK kisses VICKY. DANIEL re-enters the house.

NICK: At last *(VICKY laughs, recognising the song.)*

VICKY: At last...

NICK: My love has come along *(Singing the tune.)* du, du, du du

NICK has his arms around VICKY. He mainly, occasionally helped by her, sings, laughs and cries through 'At Last' by Etta James. After a while he starts half dancing her around the room. DANIEL hesitates outside his door for a moment and then goes in to face LEONIE. DELILAH goes to go upstairs and bumps into EMMA G who looks embarrassed and they walk away from each other.

SCENE THREE

Sunday 11am. DELILAH sits outside DANIEL's bedroom. He storms out and trips over her.

DELILAH: Daniel!

DANIEL: Fucking hell can you mind where you sit?

DELILAH: That hurt

LEONIE: *(Following out.)* Daniel...

DANIEL: Can you both stop, stop bleating out my name and both of you leave me alone

LEONIE: What's *she* done Daniel? You can't take your temper out on everyone around you she is just a kid

DELILAH: Don't say that

LEONIE: What?

DELILAH: I'm not a kid

LEONIE: Oh yes it's your birthday today isn't it? Sorry we're shouting...

DELILAH: Daniel?

DANIEL: What?

LEONIE: Daniel it's her...

DELILAH: I want to talk to you

DANIEL: Go away, go play with your friends

DELILAH: Shut up

LEONIE: *(With sympathy.)* It's her birthday!

DELILAH: Shut up, shut up you bitch

DANIEL: Start on her why don't you?

LEONIE: Delilah...

DELILAH: Shut up

DANIEL: Don't talk to her like that

DELILAH: Well you get her to fucking shut up then

DANIEL: Why? Why should I? So I can listen to your shit?

DELILAH: It's not shit Daniel for fuck's sake

LEONIE: What's going on?

DANIEL: Shut up

DELILAH: I want to talk to you

DANIEL: Well you can't, just leave me alone for God's sake

LEONIE: Daniel what the fuck...

DANIEL: Shut up I told you to shut up

DELILAH: You're such a bastard

DANIEL: Right I'm leaving now, I can't stay in this house anymore

LEONIE: Danny...

DANIEL: *(Turns on her almost about to hit her.)* Can you just, oh my God just s... *(Turns again to leave.)*

DELILAH: Daniel you can't

DANIEL: Watch me

DELILAH: You can't

DANIEL: I will

DELILAH: Please Daniel

DANIEL: Don't

DELILAH: *(Tries to take hold of his hand.)* Please

DANIEL: Fuck off

LEONIE: Look he's coming back stop getting so upset

DELILAH: Fuck off! Daniel please

LEONIE: Danny look come here

DANIEL: Shut up can you both just leave me alone!

LEONIE: Danny...look Delilah go away let me and...

DELILAH: Shut up you don't know anything

LEONIE: I know a lot more than...

DELILAH: Come back here Daniel

> *DANIEL storms into his room followed by the girls. He starts grabbing his things.*

DELILAH: Stop it Daniel

LEONIE: Danny what are you doing? Look Danny

DANIEL: Fuck off

LEONIE: Danny she's obviously got a crush on you and she's upset...

DELILAH: Shut up you don't understand anything you bitch

LEONIE: Please go away Delilah

DANIEL: No I'm going away it's fine

DELILAH: I'll do it Daniel

> *DELILAH and DANIEL are looking at each other. LEONIE takes advantage of the silence.*

LEONIE: Look everyone just calm down. Delilah just let me sort this out for a sec and Danny stop shouting at her she hasn't done anything wrong and she is only a kid so sto...

DELILAH: I'll do it

DANIEL: Leave me alone can you all just please *(Sits on the bed head in hands.)* leave

LEONIE: Daniel what on earth...

DELILAH: Daniel I mean it

LEONIE: Shut up

DELILAH: I will, I swear

LEONIE: What are you talking about?

DELILAH: I give you till ten Daniel

DANIEL: Give me five do it now, I don't give a fuck Del, I don't give a fuck

DELILAH: Really?

DANIEL: Do what you want

LEONIE: Do what?

Pause.

DELILAH: Mum!

In one stride DANIEL is standing and holding DELILAH.

LEONIE: What are you doing?

DELILAH: So you do care?

DANIEL: Delilah please

LEONIE: Get off her Danny

DELILAH: Then stay

LEONIE: What is wrong with you kid?

DELILAH: You can't go

LEONIE: Danny stop it she's only little *(Trying to push DANIEL away from DELILAH.)*

DELILAH: Please...I'll do anything

Pause, DANIEL is looking at DELILAH for a second then he grabs a bag and runs out of the room.

DELILAH: Danny! Danny! I wasn't going to, I wouldn't

LEONIE: Daniel!

LEONIE goes to follow but NICK and VICKY enter blocking her.

NICK: What the hell is going on up here?

LEONIE: *(Turning on DELILAH.)* Can you tell me what the fuck is going on?

VICKY: Don't talk to her like that

LEONIE: Sorry

VICKY: How dare you swear at my child?

NICK: Heard a hell of a racket you all yelling your heads off

VICKY: What's happened?

NICK: Where was Daniel going?

LEONIE: Delilah?

NICK: Delilah?

VICKY: Delilah?

Pause, DELILAH sits down on the bed and stares at the floor.

VICKY: Sweetheart what's wrong?

LEONIE: What's been going on?

VICKY: Can you stop bombarding her?

LEONIE: I'm sorry but you don't understand what was going on

NICK: How about you tell us Le...Leo... *(Trying to remember her name.)* Leonie

LEONIE: Me and Danny were arguing then she came up here and they started yelling at each other

VICKY: Del?

NICK: Why were you arguing with him darling you and Daniel always get on so well

LEONIE: She obviously has a crush on him

NICK: Oh don't be stupid

VICKY: It's not this new boyfriend upsetting you is it?

NICK: Christ

LEONIE: Mr...Nick?

NICK: What?

LEONIE: She has a crush on Daniel

NICK: She's far too young

LEONIE: Well if she's got a boyfriend...

VICKY: Oh honestly look *(Turning to DELILAH.)* you don't do you Del? You and Daniel are friends aren't you?

NICK: You don't think like that do you?

VICKY: Sweetheart do you like Daniel?

LEONIE: She was being very rude to me earlier...

VICKY: You have a little crush on Daniel?

NICK: Delilah do us all a favour and answer your mother

DELILAH starts crying.

NICK: Oh there's no need to cry sweetheart

VICKY: Shall we leave it for today, let's get your birthday over with

LEONIE: Why was she shouting at Danny then?

VICKY: I'm sure Daniel won't mind

LEONIE: Why was he leaving?

VICKY: What?

LEONIE: He was just saying that he was leaving

NICK: Maybe you should leave us to it sweetheart

LEONIE: But, but I don't understand what's going on

VICKY: Delilah say something darling

NICK: Yes do

VICKY: I'm sure we can sort this all out

NICK: I heard some cars in the drive your friends will be here soon

VICKY: You don't want to be upset when they turn up do you

NICK: Yes let's get this sorted out

VICKY: Come on sweetheart what on earth's being going on

NICK and VICKY both have an arm around DELILAH.

DELILAH: I told him on Friday that I liked him, he was being sweet but then I said I would say that he'd, done something to me if he left, he wants to go home because he has a family problem, that's why we're arguing...sorry

LEONIE: What family thing?

DELILAH: I dunno

LEONIE: What were you going to say he'd done?

DELILAH: I dunno. I'm sorry *(She starts crying again, LEONIE softens slightly.)*

LEONIE: Now don't cry about it, not on your birthday. That was a very mean thing to do but it's okay.

DELILAH: I'm sorry

LEONIE: *(Puts her arm around DELILAH.)* You've said the truth now haven't you, that's the most important thing

DELILAH: *(To NICK and VICKY who have drawn back.)* I'm really, really sorry

VICKY: That's disgusting Delilah

NICK: Why would you think like that?

LEONIE: It's just kids

VICKY: You've made me feel really sick Delilah

NICK: So you don't have a boyfriend

DELILAH shakes her head, both parents have stood up and away from her they move together, the door bell rings, voices can be heard from outside.

LEONIE: It's just kids see stuff on the TV and things, they don't realise what they are doing

VICKY: He's been nothing but nice to you Delilah

NICK: Don't know many other students that would put up with a little girl hanging around them all the time

VICKY: To turn that against him in such a, such a...

NICK: How can you, you're only a child!

VICKY: You're not acting much like one

NICK: Think we've been underestimating you Delilah

VICKY: *(To LEONIE.)* I'm sorry that I shouted at you before, I just never thought that...

LEONIE: She obviously didn't realise how serious this could be

NICK: That could ruin his life I hope you realise

VICKY: I feel like I don't know you

NICK: Beginning of the terrible teens

VICKY: Nick for God's sake

Doorbell rings again louder.

VICKY: Delilah since when have you been a liar?

NICK: No wonder the poor lad was upset

VICKY: You do realise what you were saying, what that would have meant? Or are you just stupid? Or sick?

NICK: It's like something you'd see on the news, why? Why would you...

VICKY: You were our little girl Delilah

NICK: We've let you have so much freedom thought you were friends with him and you just manipulate and lie to us?

VICKY: I can't look at you Del I feel so...so...

NICK: Here we were trying to defend you and you can come out with sick lies like that

LEONIE: She didn't though

VICKY: No it's worse than that! It wasn't some spur of the moment thing, you have been trying to hold it over him as blackmail

NICK: To what? What did you say before? To stop him going home to help his family

VICKY: What kind of person do you want to be Delilah?

LEONIE: She's too young to realise what she's done

NICK: Well you're thirteen today aren't you Del you're not a kid, that's what you want isn't it? To be a grown up?

VICKY: Then you have to take responsibility for your own actions

The doorbell goes again.

NICK: That's your damn friends

VICKY: Do they know what you were doing?

DELILAH shakes her head.

NICK: Well at least your friends have some idea of what is right

VICKY: And not simply sickening

NICK: Really, really disappointed in you

LEONIE: Don't be too angry with her she's just a kid

The doorbell rings again. They sing 'Hey there Delilah', trying to get her to come to the door. No one moves in the room. Blackout.

END

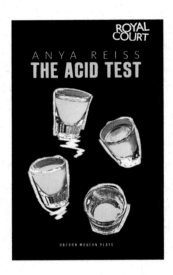

THE ACID TEST
9781849430456

'This has been the worst day of my life.
So can you please get drunk with me?'

Dana, Ruth and Jess down shots to console the heart-broken,
to comfort the anxious and just pass the time. Kicked out
from the family home Jess's dad, Jim, invades the party with
just as much recklessness as the girls. As the night passes
and vodka bottles are emptied, Friday night in becomes high
drama. An unruly new comedy asking if age equals maturity,
opened at the Royal Court in May 2011.

WWW.OBERONBOOKS.COM

Printed by Printforce, United Kingdom